Building AI Agents for Network Operations

Design LLM-powered NetOps workflows with Python, Ollama, MCP, and tool calling

Sif Baksh

<packt>

Building AI Agents for Network Operations

Portfolio Director: Kartikey Pandey
Proposal Writer: Reshma Raman
Project Manager: Sonam Pandey
Content Engineer: Arun Nadar
Technical Editor: Simran Ali
Copy Editor: Arun Nadar
Indexer: Manju Arasan
Production Designer: Aparna Bhagat

First published: July 2026

Production reference: 1150726

Published by Packt Publishing Ltd.
Grosvenor House
11 St Paul's Square
Birmingham
B3 1RB, UK.

ISBN 978-1-80834-683-5
www.packtpub.com

Contributors

About the author

Sif Baksh is a network automation architect, solutions engineer, and technical educator with more than 15 years of experience across networking, security, infrastructure, and automation. His work focuses on helping engineering teams build governed workflows that connect network data, infrastructure APIs, operational tools, and human approvals into systems that are practical, observable, and safe to operate.

His technical background includes DNS/DHCP/IPAM automation, network and security operations, threat intelligence enrichment, compliance workflows, incident response, and tool integration. He has worked with teams to replace manual, ticket-driven processes with repeatable automation patterns designed for production environments.

His current work explores how AI agents, local LLMs, prompt design, tool calling, MCP servers, and agentic troubleshooting loops can be applied to network operations without losing validation or control. Through his writing, workshops, videos, and community projects, he teaches engineers how to turn AI ideas into NetOps workflows that can be tested, reviewed, and trusted.

First and foremost, I want to thank my wife, Daneen.

Thank you for supporting me through the late nights, the long weekends, the endless experiments, and all the moments when I said, "I just need a little more time." Your encouragement made this possible, and I am grateful for you every day.

I also want to thank Eric Chou for his support and impact in the network automation community. Your work has inspired many of us to keep building, keep learning, and keep making network automation more approachable.

To everyone who has shared ideas, reviewed concepts, asked hard questions, watched the videos, attended the workshops, or cheered for me along the way, thank you. This book is the result of years of learning from the community and trying to give something useful back.

Table of Contents

Appendix A: [illegible] 177

Preface

Network operations has always been a context-heavy job. A single incident can involve alerts, command-line output, routing state, interface status, topology notes, change records, and handoffs between teams. The challenge is not just collecting information. It is knowing what to check next, how to keep the evidence clear, and how to avoid turning an investigation into guesswork.

AI agents are becoming interesting for network teams because they can help gather context, reason over evidence, and support troubleshooting workflows. But they also introduce new risks if they are given too much freedom, trusted without validation, or connected to tools without clear controls. This book takes a careful, engineering-led view of AI in network operations. The goal is not to replace network engineers or automate blindly. The goal is to show how AI-assisted workflows can support engineers while keeping validation, visibility, and control at the center.

Building AI Agents for Network Operations starts with local large language model workflows and gradually builds toward a controlled troubleshooting agent. You will work with prompts, structured output, memory, tool calling, MCP, and production-readiness patterns. Each part of the journey is designed to help you understand not only what the agent does, but also how the surrounding application keeps it safe and useful.

By the end of this book, you should have a clear path for designing, testing, and reviewing AI-assisted network workflows that can move from a local lab toward controlled operational evaluation.

Who this book is for

This book is for network engineers, NetOps engineers, NOC engineers, SREs, DevOps engineers, network automation professionals, and platform engineers who want to understand how AI agents can support network troubleshooting and operations. If you work with CLI output, routing issues, incident triage, automation scripts, or operational tooling, this book will help you connect AI concepts to familiar network workflows. Basic networking knowledge and comfort with the command line will help you get the most from the examples. Beginner-level Python knowledge is useful, but the labs are designed to explain the important application patterns as they are introduced.

What this book covers

Chapter 1, Understanding AI Agents for Network Operations, introduces what AI agents mean in a NetOps context. It explains the difference between chatbots, copilots, automation scripts, and agents, and shows where agents can help with investigation, context gathering, and operational decision support.

Chapter 2, LLM Fundamentals and Local Setup, explains the large language model concepts that matter most for network engineers, including tokens, context windows, temperature, stateless calls, and local model execution. It also helps you set up Ollama, Python, and the book lab environment.

Chapter 3, Prompt Engineering for Network Automation, shows how to write prompts that are reliable enough for repeatable NetOps tasks. It introduces a simple RACE prompt structure and applies it to parsing, alert triage, documentation, and troubleshooting examples.

Chapter 4, Parsing Network Outputs into Structured Data, shows how to convert raw CLI output into validated JSON. It uses interface status, BGP summaries, multi-vendor examples, malformed data, and validation checks to prepare network data for automation and agent workflows.

Chapter 5, Building a Network Chatbot with Memory, builds a chatbot that can retain troubleshooting context across turns. It explains why memory belongs in the application layer and shows how conversation history, system prompts, and context management shape model behavior.

Chapter 6, Designing Tools and Agentic Workflows, introduces tool calling and shows how a chatbot becomes an agent. It covers mock network tools, approved function mapping, input validation, loop limits, failure handling, logging, and safe tool execution.

Chapter 7, Building the Main Network Troubleshooting Agent, brings the earlier pieces together into a realistic troubleshooting workflow. You will run the Lab 4 agent, investigate device status, BGP health, interface state, reachability, and use evidence to review the agent response before trusting it.

Chapter 8, From Lab Agents to Reusable Tools with MCP, moves from direct tool calling to reusable tool packaging with MCP. It introduces safe network wrappers, an MCP server, an HTTP bridge, and a browser UI for testing reusable network tools across clients.

Chapter 9, Moving Toward Production-Ready Network Agents, focuses on what changes when an agent moves from a lab to a controlled operational review. It covers read-only first design, authentication, authorization, secrets, validation, logging, approvals, observability, rollback planning, runbooks, feature flags, support ownership, and go/no-go reviews.

Appendix A, AI Network Agent Design Toolkit, provides reusable worksheets and checklists for use-case scoring, prompt review, structured-output validation, memory policy, tool safety, MCP contracts, evidence records, pilot readiness, runbooks, feature flags, and final operational review.

To get the most out of this book

To follow along with the examples in this book, you will need a local development environment that can run Python, Ollama, and the repository labs. The main learning path uses mocked network data, so you do not need access to production devices or a live network lab to complete the book.

Before you begin, make sure you have the following:

- Python 3.10 or later installed on your system
- Git installed so you can clone the book repository
- Ollama installed for running local models
- The `llama3.2:3b` model for the early labs
- The `deepseek-r1:8b` model for the agentic troubleshooting lab
- A code editor such as Visual Studio Code or another editor of your choice
- A terminal or command prompt for running the lab commands
- A modern browser for the MCP browser UI in *Chapter 8*
- Basic familiarity with routing, interfaces, BGP, CLI output, and troubleshooting workflows

The examples are designed to be followed in order. You will get the best value if you clone the repository, create the Python virtual environment, install the dependencies, and run each lab as it appears in the chapters. The book keeps live network access optional and outside the main learning path so you can focus on the agent patterns, safety controls, and review process before adapting the ideas to your own environment. The repository also includes editable versions of the *Appendix A* design artifacts under `docs/design-toolkit/`.

Some labs use local LLMs, so model speed and response quality may vary depending on your system resources. If a model response differs slightly from the example output, focus on whether the workflow, validation, and evidence are correct.

The labs in this book use specific local models so that the examples remain consistent and easier to follow. As local LLMs continue to improve, you can also try the same prompts, parsing tasks, and agent workflows with other models in the future. When you do this, compare the outputs carefully, validate structured results, and keep the same safety checks before using any model output in an operational workflow.

Download the example code files

The code bundle for the book is hosted on GitHub at `https://github.com/PacktPublishing/Building-AI-Agents-for-Network-Operations`. We also have other code bundles from our rich catalog of books and videos available at `https://github.com/PacktPublishing`. Check them out!

Download the color images

We also provide a PDF file that has color images of the screenshots/diagrams used in this book. You can download it here: `https://packt.link/gbp/9781808346835`.

Conventions used

There are a number of text conventions used throughout this book.

Code in text: Indicates code words in text, folder names, filenames, file extensions, pathnames, commands, user input, and tool names. For example: "The lab files include `labs/lab5-mcp/mcp_server.py`, `http_bridge.py`, and `ui.html`."

A block of code is set as follows:

```
from mcp.server.fastmcp import FastMCP

mcp = FastMCP("network-agent-tools")

@mcp.tool()
def bgp_summary(device: str) -> dict:
    """Get BGP neighbor summary for a lab network device."""
    return safe_bgp_summary(device)
```

Any command-line input or output is written as follows:

```
ollama pull deepseek-r1:8b
python3 labs/lab4-agentic/agentic_network_bot_ollama.py
```

Bold: Indicates a new term, an important word, or words that you see on the screen. For instance, a new term appears like this: **Model Context Protocol (MCP)** gives us a cleaner way to expose tools to clients.

> **Note**
>
> Warnings or important notes appear like this.

> **Tip**
>
> Tips and tricks appear like this.

Get in touch

Feedback from our readers is always welcome.

General feedback: If you have questions about any aspect of this book or have any general feedback, please email us at `customercare@packt.com` and mention the book's title in the subject of your message.

Errata: Although we have taken every care to ensure the accuracy of our content, mistakes do happen. If you have found a mistake in this book, we would be grateful if you reported this to us. Please visit `https://www.packt.com/submit-errata`, click **Submit Errata**, and fill in the form.

Piracy: If you come across any illegal copies of our works in any form on the internet, we would be grateful if you would provide us with the location address or website name. Please contact us at `copyright@packt.com` with a link to the material.

If you are interested in becoming an author: If there is a topic that you have expertise in and you are interested in either writing or contributing to a book, please visit .

Share your thoughts

Once you've read *Building AI Agents for Network Operations*, we'd love to hear your thoughts! Scan the QR code below to go straight to the Amazon review page for this book and share your feedback.

https://packt.link/r/1-808-34683-1

Your review is important to us and the tech community and will help us make sure we're delivering excellent quality content.

Free benefits with your book

This book comes with free benefits to support your learning. Activate them now for instant access (see the "*How to Unlock*" section for instructions).

Here's a quick overview of what you can instantly unlock with your purchase:

DRM-Free PDF Version

Download DRM-free PDF and ePub copies of this book.

7-Day Packt Library Access

Get 7-day unlimited access to 8,000+ books and videos. No credit card required.

Available for first-time Packt+ trial users only.

Next-Gen Reader Access

Read this book on Packt Reader with progress sync, dark mode and note-taking.

How to Unlock

Scan the QR code (or go to `packtpub.com/unlock`). Search for this book by name, confirm the edition, and then follow the steps on the page.

UNLOCK NOW

Note: Keep your invoice handy. Purchases made directly from Packt don't require an invoice.

Stay Sharp in Cloud and DevOps – Join 44,000+ Subscribers of CloudPro

CloudPro is a weekly newsletter for cloud professionals who want to stay current on the fast-evolving world of cloud computing, DevOps, and infrastructure engineering.

Every issue delivers focused, high-signal content on topics like:

- AWS, GCP & multi-cloud architecture
- Containers, Kubernetes & orchestration
- Infrastructure as Code (IaC) with Terraform, Pulumi, etc.
- Platform engineering & automation workflows
- Observability, performance tuning, and reliability best practices

Whether you're a cloud engineer, SRE, DevOps practitioner, or platform lead, CloudPro helps you stay on top of what matters, without the noise.

Scan the QR code to join for free and get weekly insights straight to your inbox:

1

Understanding AI Agents for Network Operations

Most network engineers do not wake up thinking about **agents**, **tokens**, or **model context windows**. They wake up thinking about why **Border Gateway Protocol (BGP)** is down, why an alert fired, why a change caused pain, or why a ticket says the application is slow but nobody can agree where the problem lives.

That is the reality of network operations. The job is not just about routers, switches, firewalls, and links. It is about collecting scattered clues, sorting through noisy signals, checking live state, and making a decision before the business feels the impact. Some days that means staring at dashboards. Some days it means reading logs. Some days it means running the same command across ten devices because one of them is lying to you.

This is where **artificial intelligence (AI) agents** start to become interesting. Not because they are magical. Not because they replace engineers. And definitely not because every workflow suddenly needs AI bolted onto it. The useful version is much more practical: an AI agent can help collect context, parse messy output, choose the right tool, summarize what happened, and give the engineer a faster starting point.

That distinction matters. A chatbot that answers *What is BGP?* is useful for learning. An agent that can inspect interface state, check BGP neighbors, review logs, and explain what it found is a different kind of system. It is still software. It still needs boundaries. But it can support operational work in a way that a plain chat interface cannot.

In this chapter, we will set the foundation for the rest of the book by looking at what AI agents are, where they fit in network operations, and where they should be used carefully. The goal is not hype. The goal is to understand what we are building, why it matters, and how to think about agents as controlled systems that support engineers rather than replace them.

In this chapter, we will cover the following topics:

- Define AI agents in a **network operations (NetOps)** context
- Compare agents, chatbots, copilots, and automation
- Identify practical use cases for AI agents in network operations
- Recognize where traditional automation remains the better choice
- Understand the role of tools, context, validation, and guardrails
- Preview the agent journey we will build throughout this book

Technical requirements

This chapter does not require any technical setup, lab files, or software installation. It is a conceptual chapter that establishes the vocabulary, operating boundaries, and safety mindset we will use before the hands-on work begins. With that clear, we can start with the operational problem agents are trying to solve.

The operational problem agents are trying to solve

Network operations has always been a **context problem**. The device tells you one thing. The monitoring system tells you another. The ticket says users are affected, but the dashboard looks green. Someone changed something, but the change record is vague. A route is missing, but the interface is up. An alert says critical, but the actual impact is unclear.

None of that is new. What has changed is the amount of data and the speed at which teams are expected to respond. Modern environments generate more telemetry, more logs, more alerts, and more change events than most teams can manually process in real time. When everything is noisy, the hard part is not finding data. The hard part is finding the right data and turning it into a decision.

Traditional dashboards help, but they still require a human to jump between views and mentally stitch the story together. **Traditional automation** helps, but only when the workflow is known and predictable. If the problem is always the same, a script can handle it. If the problem requires investigation, correlation, and judgment, the workflow becomes harder to encode as simple *if this, then that* logic.

This is the space where agents can help. An agent can be given a goal, such as *investigate why this BGP neighbor is down*. It can reason about what information it needs, call safe tools, inspect the results, and return a summary with evidence. The engineer still decides what to do next. The agent simply helps reduce the time spent collecting and organizing the first round of context.

That sounds simple, but it matters. A good starting point during an incident can save minutes. Sometimes minutes matter. Even when they do not, reducing repetitive investigation work makes engineers more consistent and less dependent on tribal knowledge.

> **Note**
>
> In this book, we treat AI agents as **operational assistants**. They help gather context, reason over evidence, and support decisions. They do not get unlimited access to the network, and they do not blindly change configurations.

Now that we have framed the operational problem, we need to define what we actually mean by an agent. That definition matters because the word is often used too loosely.

What is an AI agent?

The word **agent** is doing a lot of work right now. Depending on who you ask, it can mean anything from a chatbot with a better prompt to a system that can plan, call tools, and support operational decisions. That ambiguity is part of the problem. Before we build anything, we need a working definition that is useful for network operations.

For this book, an AI agent is a software system that uses a **language model**, **application code**, **tools**, **context**, and **guardrails** to help complete a task. The language model provides reasoning and language understanding. The code provides structure. The tools provide controlled access to data or actions. The context gives the agent information about the environment. The guardrails define what the agent is allowed to do.

Here, **large language model (LLM)** refers to the model that understands and generates language. We will use LLM throughout the rest of the book.

A practical way to remember this is: *agent = LLM + code + tools + context + guardrails.*

The model alone is not the agent. A model can generate text, but it does not magically know the current state of your routers. It does not know whether *Ethernet1* is down right now. It does not know whether a BGP neighbor is established unless we give it that data.

That is where the agent architecture matters. It gives the model a controlled way to understand the request, decide what information is needed, call an approved tool, inspect the result, and build a response that is grounded in evidence.

Figure 1.1 shows this basic flow. The important thing to notice is that the LLM is only one part of the system. The useful behavior comes from combining reasoning, safe tool access, network state, and guardrails:

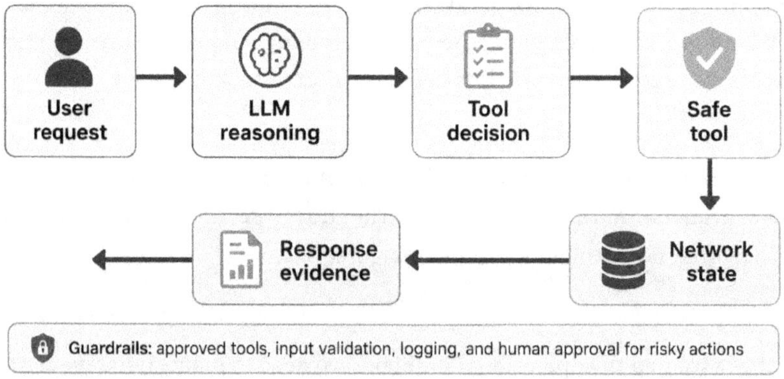

Figure 1.1: Basic AI agent architecture with controlled tool execution

This is where things get interesting. Once we stop treating the LLM as an all-knowing box and start treating it as one component inside an engineered workflow, we can build something useful. We can define narrow tools, validate inputs, log activity, restrict actions, and keep humans in control. That is very different from pasting a config into a chat window and hoping for the best.

Now that the basic architecture is clear, we can separate agents from the other tools they are often confused with.

Chatbots, copilots, automation, and agents

One reason teams get confused is that several AI and automation patterns look similar from the outside. A **chatbot** can answer questions. A **copilot** can help a user write code or understand output. A **script** can automate a fixed workflow. An **agent** can use tools and context to work through a task. These systems can overlap, but they are not the same thing.

The difference matters because it affects how we build, test, operate, and trust the system. A chatbot that explains BGP route selection has a different risk profile from an agent that can connect to a device. A script that runs a known command has a different failure mode from an agent that chooses which tool to call based on a prompt.

Table 1.1 compares these patterns at a practical level so we can be clear about what each one is good at and where each one needs care:

System type	**What it does well**	**Where it needs care**
Chatbot	Explains concepts and summarizes provided text	Does not know live state unless you provide it
Copilot	Helps a human write code, prompts, or documentation	Still depends on the user to drive the workflow
Automation script	Runs fixed logic with predictable inputs	Struggles when the next step depends on changing context
AI agent	Uses tools and context to support investigation	Needs validation, logging, permissions, and human oversight

Table 1.1: Comparing chatbots, copilots, automation scripts, and AI agents

A lot of frustration comes from using the wrong pattern for the job. If you need to run the same command every hour and compare the result against a threshold, a normal automation script is probably the right answer. If you need to explain a protocol to a junior engineer, a chatbot may be enough. If you need to investigate a messy operational event where the next step depends on what you find, an agent starts to make sense.

Here is the part people usually skip: an agent is not automatically better than automation. It is different. Traditional automation is excellent when the workflow is known. Agents are useful when the workflow requires observation, tool selection, reasoning, and summarization. The trick is knowing which situation you are in.

That distinction gives us a useful filter. Instead of asking whether agents are good or bad, we can ask where they actually help.

Where agents help in network operations

Network teams already have plenty of tools. The problem is not a lack of tools. The problem is that tools often produce isolated pieces of information. One system has alerts. Another has logs. Another has inventory. Another has configuration. The engineer becomes the integration layer, moving between systems and mentally building the timeline.

Agents can help when the work involves pulling together multiple pieces of context. The agent does not need to know everything. It needs safe ways to retrieve the right things at the right time. That may mean calling a function that returns interface status, asking another tool for BGP neighbors, checking recent logs, and then summarizing what changed.

The most useful early agent use cases tend to be *read only*. That is intentional. Before we let an agent change anything, we need to trust how it observes. Read only agents can still provide a lot of value without increasing operational risk. They can summarize, classify, extract, correlate, and recommend.

Alert triage

Alert triage is a strong first use case because alerts rarely arrive with enough context. An alert may say that a BGP session is down, but the engineer still needs to know which device is involved, whether the interface is up, whether the peer is reachable, whether there were recent errors, and whether the event is new or part of a larger pattern.

An agent can help by enriching the alert. It can collect current state, summarize the likely impact, and suggest the next checks. It does not need to close the incident. It just needs to reduce the first few minutes of manual searching.

CLI output parsing

A lot of network automation dies on messy input. **Command Line Interface (CLI)** output is not always clean **JavaScript Object Notation (JSON)**. It may be vendor-specific, inconsistent, wrapped oddly, or missing fields. Humans are surprisingly good at reading this kind of output. Scripts are not always as forgiving.

LLMs can help parse unstructured or semi-structured output into a more useful format, such as JSON. That does not mean we blindly trust the result. It means we can use the model to help normalize the output, then validate the result before passing it downstream. This is one of the core patterns we will build later in the book.

Troubleshooting support

Troubleshooting is rarely one question and one answer. It is a trail of clues. You check the interface. Then you check the neighbor. Then you check logs. Then you compare the current state with what you expected. Then you ask whether this is a device problem, a link problem, a routing problem, or something upstream.

An agent can follow that trail in a controlled way. It can call tools, inspect results, and decide what to check next. That is different from a static script that always runs the same steps. The agent can adapt based on the evidence it receives.

Documentation and handoffs

Documentation and handoffs are two areas where operational knowledge often gets lost. Network state changes. Diagrams drift. Runbooks get stale. Troubleshooting notes live in tickets, chats, and someone's memory.

Agents can help turn structured topology data, command outputs, and incident notes into readable documentation. They can generate summaries for handoffs, explain what was checked, and highlight what remains unknown. Again, the value is not magic. The value is reducing the manual copy and paste work that usually gets skipped during busy operations.

These use cases keep the agent close to observation, summarization, and recommendation. That is the safest place to start. The next question is just as important: where should we avoid using agents?

Where agents are the wrong tool

This is where we need to be honest. Not every workflow needs an agent. Some workflows should never start with an agent. If the task is deterministic, well understood, and already handled reliably by a script or platform, do not make it more complicated just because AI is available.

I like asking a simple question before adding AI: *is AI actually helping here?* If the answer is no, stop. That does not make the solution less modern. It makes it sane.

For example, if you need to check whether a device responds to *ping* every minute, use normal monitoring. If you need to archive configs nightly, use automation. If you need to enforce a known policy, use deterministic checks. If you need to approve a production configuration change, keep a human in the loop.

> **Tip**
>
> If a basic script solves the problem reliably, use the script. Save agents for problems where context, uncertainty, summarization, or tool selection actually matter.

Agents introduce their own operational concerns. The model can misunderstand a prompt. It can produce output in the wrong format. It can ask for a tool with invalid parameters. It can summarize confidently and still miss something important. None of this makes agents useless. It just means we need to design them like engineers, not like marketers.

That means **safe defaults**. It means input validation. It means structured outputs. It means logging every tool call. It means failing closed when something looks wrong. It means read-only first. Always.

The basic agent workflow

Now that we have defined what an agent is made of, the next step is to look at how it behaves during a basic troubleshooting flow. We do not need a complex architecture yet. We just need a clear mental model for how the pieces work together.

At a high level, a useful agent workflow is not complicated. The user asks a question or submits a problem. The agent observes the request, reasons about what it needs, takes the next allowed step, validates the result, and then reports back to the user. If the next step could change the network, the workflow should stop and ask for human approval first.

In network operations, this is what makes the system practical. One tool might return interface status. Another might return BGP neighbor information. Another might search logs or check reachability. The language model is not running random commands on its own. Your code controls execution. The model helps decide what information is needed, and your application decides whether the next step is allowed.

Figure 1.2 shows this workflow in a simple form. The main idea is that the agent does not jump straight from a question to an action. It follows a controlled sequence: *observe, reason, act, validate*, and *report*. Validation happens before the final response, and risky actions still require human approval:

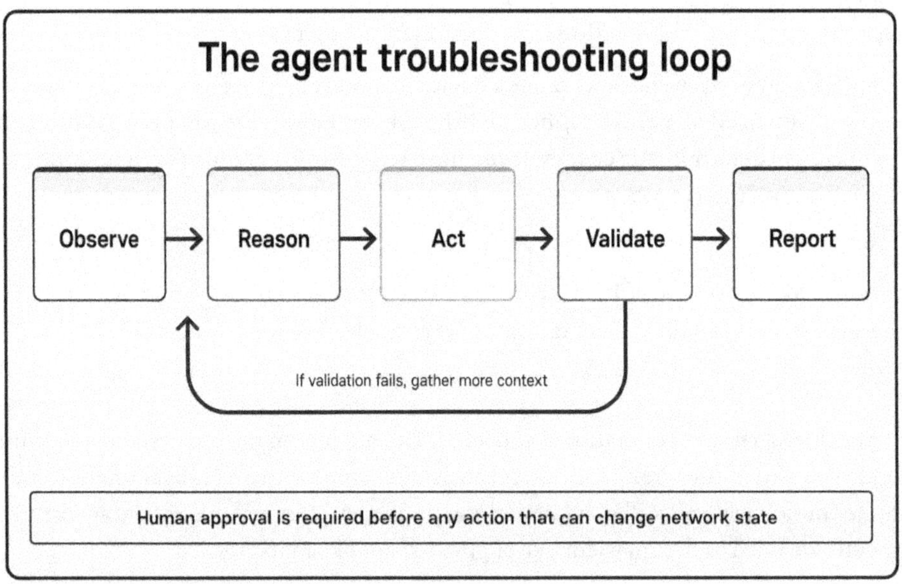

Figure 1.2: Agent workflow with validation and human approval boundaries

This separation matters. The model is the reasoning and language layer. Your application code is the execution layer. Your tools define the operating boundaries. Validation checks whether the result makes sense. Logging helps you understand what happened. Human approval keeps risky actions under control.

A good agent is only as good as the tools and boundaries around it. If the tools are poorly described, the agent may call them incorrectly. If the outputs are messy, the answer will be messy. If validation is missing, bad data can move through the workflow. If logging is missing, troubleshooting the agent can become harder than troubleshooting the network itself.

That gives us the general shape of the workflow. To make it more concrete, let us place the same pattern inside a common network operations scenario.

A practical troubleshooting scenario

Let us make this less abstract. Imagine a **Network Operations Center (NOC)** engineer receives an alert that says a BGP neighbor is down on a core router. The alert itself is not enough. The engineer needs to know whether the peer is reachable, whether the local interface is up, whether there are errors, whether the route table changed, and whether logs show a recent flap.

In a traditional workflow, the engineer may jump between the monitoring platform, the device CLI, a log tool, a ticket, and maybe an inventory system. That is normal, but it is also repetitive. If the same investigation happens every week, we can reduce some of the manual work.

A simple agent-assisted workflow might follow these steps:

1. Receive the alert text and extract key details, such as device name, peer address, and severity
2. Call a read-only tool to check the current BGP neighbor state
3. Call another tool to inspect the relevant interface status and error counters
4. Search recent logs for neighbor reset messages or interface changes
5. Summarize the evidence and identify likely causes
6. Return suggested next steps for the engineer to validate

Notice what the agent is not doing. It is not blindly changing configuration. It is not resetting a session without approval. It is not deciding business impact on its own. It is collecting evidence and helping the engineer move faster.

This is the pattern we will build toward in this book. We will start with small pieces: local LLM calls, structured prompts, parsing output, memory, and tools. Then we will combine those pieces into an agent that can support network troubleshooting.

That brings us to one of the most important design principles in the book: the engineer stays in control.

Human control is not optional

There is a lot of marketing around **self healing networks** and **self driving networks**. Some of it is useful. Some of it is noise. In real network environments, especially in production, accountability still matters. Someone owns the change. Someone owns the outage. Someone has to explain what happened.

That is why **human control** is not a side feature. It is part of the architecture. A read-only investigation agent can run with fewer concerns because it is only collecting and summarizing data. A write-capable agent is different. Before anything changes on a device, the system needs approval, audit trails, rollback planning, and clear boundaries.

This book will keep that line clear. We will build agents that can help investigate. We will discuss what changes when you move toward production. We will talk about secrets, **role based access control (RBAC)**, logging, observability, retries, validation, and approval workflows. The goal is not to build something flashy. The goal is to build something an operations team could eventually trust.

Keeping humans in control does not mean ignoring automation. It means using automation carefully, and that is where traditional automation and agents start to work together.

How traditional automation and agents work together

Agents do not replace automation. They sit beside it, and in many cases they depend on it. This is where traditional automation and AI start to meet.

A workflow automation platform might already know how to open a ticket, enrich an alert, query an **application programming interface (API)**, or send a message to an on-call engineer. An agent can use those capabilities as tools. The automation layer handles deterministic work. The agent layer helps with reasoning, summarization, and deciding what context to collect next.

This is a healthier way to think about agent design. Do not throw away working automation. Wrap it. Expose safe parts of it as tools. Let the agent request context through controlled interfaces. Keep the pieces that are deterministic as deterministic as possible.

For example, a script that collects interface status should stay a script. The agent does not need to reinvent that. The agent needs to know when to call it, what result came back, and how that result changes the investigation.

Once we think about agents this way, the rest of the book becomes easier to follow. We are not building one giant system all at once. We are building the pieces that make this kind of controlled workflow possible.

What you will build in this book

This book is a build journey. We are not going to start with a giant agent and hope it works. We will build the pieces one at a time so you understand what each part does and where it can break.

The path looks like this:

- Run local LLMs with **Ollama** so you can experiment without sending data to a cloud API
- Learn the LLM fundamentals that matter for network work, including tokens, context, temperature, and memory
- Write prompts that produce consistent structured outputs for parsing, triage, and documentation
- Convert raw network command output into JSON that later tools and workflows can use
- Build a chatbot that remembers troubleshooting context across multiple turns
- Design safe tools that expose network state without giving the model unlimited access
- Build an agentic troubleshooting loop that can reason, call tools, validate results, and report findings
- Package reusable tools with **Model Context Protocol (MCP)** so they can be shared beyond one application
- Move from mock devices toward production-aware design with logging, approvals, secrets, and observability

By the end, you should understand how to build a practical NetOps agent that can inspect network state, work through common troubleshooting paths, and produce useful summaries for an engineer. More importantly, you should understand the boundaries. You will know why validation matters, why read-only first is the right starting point, and why human approval is required before risky actions.

That understanding is more valuable than a one-off demo. Demos are easy. Systems that survive contact with real operations are harder.

Before we move into the hands-on chapters, we should also set expectations about what production readiness really means.

Production reality check

Before we go further, let us set expectations. The first versions of the agents we build will use local models and mock data. That is intentional. Mock data gives us a safe place to learn the pattern without risking a production device. It also makes the labs repeatable for every reader.

When we move toward real devices, the architecture needs to grow up a little. A production aware agent needs more than a good prompt. It needs credentials handled properly. It needs input validation. It needs timeouts and retries. It needs structured error messages. It needs logs. It needs observability. It needs a way to prove what it did and why.

Here are the production ideas we will return to throughout the book:

- Start with read-only tools and prove the agent can observe accurately
- Validate every tool input before executing anything
- Return structured outputs so downstream logic can check the result
- Log all tool calls, arguments, results, errors, and execution times
- Store secrets outside the code and never print sensitive values
- Use RBAC so tools expose only what each user or workflow should access
- Require human approval for any action that changes the network
- Test failure cases, not just happy paths

These are not advanced topics for later because we want to make the book longer. They are part of building responsibly. Even in a lab, we want to build habits that carry into production.

With those expectations set, we can define what success should look like for a practical network agent.

How to think about success

A successful network agent does not have to solve every outage. That is the wrong goal. A better goal is to reduce the time it takes to get to useful context. If the agent can collect the right facts, summarize the evidence, and suggest the next few checks, it has already helped.

Success might look like this:

- The engineer receives a cleaner summary instead of raw alert noise
- The agent extracts device names, peer addresses, and interface names correctly
- The system validates JSON output before using it downstream
- The troubleshooting path is logged and repeatable

- The agent refuses to run unsafe or unsupported actions
- The final recommendation includes evidence rather than vague guesses

That last point matters. A useful operational answer should not just say, *BGP is down because the interface is down.* It should show the evidence: the interface state, the peer state, the relevant log entry, and the timestamp. Engineers trust systems that show their work.

That is the mindset we will carry forward: useful agents do not need to be dramatic. They need to be grounded, controlled, and helpful.

Summary

In this chapter, we set the foundation for the rest of the book. We looked at why AI agents are useful in network operations, especially when teams are dealing with alert noise, scattered context, and troubleshooting workflows that are difficult to express as simple scripts.

We also drew an important line. Agents are not magic, and they are not replacements for engineers. They are systems built from models, code, tools, context, and guardrails. They are most useful when they help engineers gather evidence, reason over messy information, and move faster without giving up control.

We compared chatbots, copilots, automation scripts, and agents. We also covered where agents help, where they do not belong, and why read only first is the safest starting point. That mindset will show up again and again as we move through the book.

In the next chapter, we will look under the hood of the language models that power these systems. We will cover tokens, context windows, temperature, stateless API calls, and local setup with Ollama. Once you understand how the model behaves, the rest of the agent architecture becomes much easier to reason about.

Get this book's PDF version and more

Scan the QR code (or go to `packtpub.com/unlock`). Search for this book by name, confirm the edition, and then follow the steps on the page.

UNLOCK NOW

Note: Keep your invoice handy. Purchases made directly from Packt don't require an invoice.

2

LLM Fundamentals and Local Setup

Most network engineers do not need to become **artificial intelligence (AI)** researchers. That is not the job. The job is to understand enough about **large language models (LLMs)** to use them safely, predictably, and practically in **network operations (NetOps)**.

If you have already used a chatbot, you have seen the useful side of LLMs. They can summarize logs, explain protocols, draft scripts, and help reason through messy text. But if you have also seen the same prompt produce slightly different answers, or watched a model confidently produce output in the wrong format, you have also seen the part that makes engineers nervous.

This matters for NetOps because our use cases are not just casual questions. We want to parse command output, summarize incidents, build troubleshooting assistants, and eventually let an agent call tools. Before we do any of that, we need a working mental model for how these systems behave.

In this chapter, we will keep the theory practical. We will look at tokens, context windows, temperature, stateless calls, and memory. Then we will set up **Ollama** so we can run a local model and call it from Python. By the end, you will have a local lab ready for the rest of the book.

In this chapter, we will cover the following topics:

- Review the technical requirements and local lab assumptions
- Explain how LLMs behave in network automation tasks
- Understand tokens, context windows, and stateless **application programming interface (API)** calls

- Control model behavior with temperature and response limits
- Set up Ollama and run a local model
- Call a local model from Python
- Test temperature changes and basic token behavior
- Troubleshoot common local setup issues

These topics give us the foundation we need before prompt engineering, parsing, memory, and tool calling. If Chapter 1 explained why agents matter, this chapter explains the model behavior we need to respect while building them.

Technical requirements

Before running the examples, make sure you have the basic tools installed. The fast path is available in `QUICKSTART.md`. This chapter uses the same setup path but explains why each piece matters.

You need the following tools:

- **Python** 3.10 or later
- **Git** to clone the repository
- **Ollama** to run the local model
- **Visual Studio Code (VS Code)** or another editor
- The repository dependencies from `requirements.txt`

You do not need a cloud account or an API key for this chapter. Everything we do here runs locally once the model is downloaded.

Understanding why LLM fundamentals matter for NetOps

A lot of LLM explanations either go too deep into machine learning theory or stay too high level to be useful. Neither helps much when you are trying to build a network troubleshooting workflow. We need the middle ground: enough understanding to make good engineering decisions.

For network work, the important point is that LLMs are very good at recognizing patterns in text. That makes them useful for reading logs, summarizing tickets, generating first drafts of documentation, and turning messy command output into structured data. The same strength also creates risk. A model can generate fluent text that looks right while still being wrong, incomplete, or formatted badly.

That is why we treat the model as one component in a larger system. It can help with language and reasoning, but the application still needs validation, tool boundaries, error handling, and human review where appropriate. This is the same mindset we used in Chapter 1: useful, but controlled.

Before we write prompts or build agents, we need to understand how the model receives input, generates output, and forgets context between calls. That starts with a simple question: what is an LLM actually doing?

Understanding what a large language model is

A large language model is a model trained to predict likely text based on patterns it has seen during training. That is the plain English version. It does not sit there with a routing table in its head. It does not know your live network. It generates the next likely pieces of text based on the input you provide and the patterns it has learned.

This is why LLMs can feel surprisingly useful for network tasks. If you paste a routing protocol explanation, a log snippet, or a command output, the model has likely seen similar patterns before. It can recognize structure, extract values, summarize meaning, and explain what something probably represents.

The practical warning is just as important: **pattern recognition** is not the same thing as deterministic truth. An LLM may produce a valid-looking answer without actually validating it against your environment. That is why we use it for tasks such as parsing, summarization, and assistance, while still building checks around the result.

Before writing a single prompt, this distinction can save you hours of debugging. *Table 2.1* shows where LLMs fit in NetOps work and where the surrounding system still needs to take over:

Task type	**Where an LLM helps**	**Where the system needs guardrails**
Log summarization	Condenses noisy logs into a readable summary	Validate important facts against the source data
Command output parsing	Extracts values from semi structured text	Check output against a schema before using it
Documentation drafting	Turns topology or incident notes into readable text	Review for accuracy before publishing

Task type	Where an LLM helps	Where the system needs guardrails
Configuration generation	Creates a starting point or template	Never push generated config without review and testing
Troubleshooting support	Suggests likely next checks based on evidence	Require evidence and avoid unsupported conclusions

Table 2.1: Where LLMs help in NetOps and where guardrails are still required

The pattern should look familiar. We want to use the model where it is strong, then wrap it with validation where the outcome matters. That approach becomes easier once we understand how the model sees text.

Working with tokens and context windows

LLMs do not process text exactly the way humans read words. They process text as **tokens**. A token is a chunk of text. Sometimes it is a whole word. Sometimes it is part of a word. Sometimes it is punctuation or spacing. You do not need to become obsessed with token math, but you do need to know that every prompt and every response consumes tokens.

This matters because network data gets large quickly. A small prompt such as `show ip interface brief` is tiny. A full device configuration, a long log file, or command output from a large spine-leaf environment can become large very quickly. If you also include conversation history, examples, schemas, and instructions, the context can grow faster than expected.

The **context window** is the amount of text the model can consider at one time. Think of it as the working area available to the model for the current request. If the useful information is inside the window, the model can use it. If it is missing, truncated, or buried under too much irrelevant data, the response can degrade.

The basic idea is shown in *Figure 2.1*. We send text into the model, the text is broken into tokens, and those tokens fit inside a context window. The model then generates output tokens as the response:

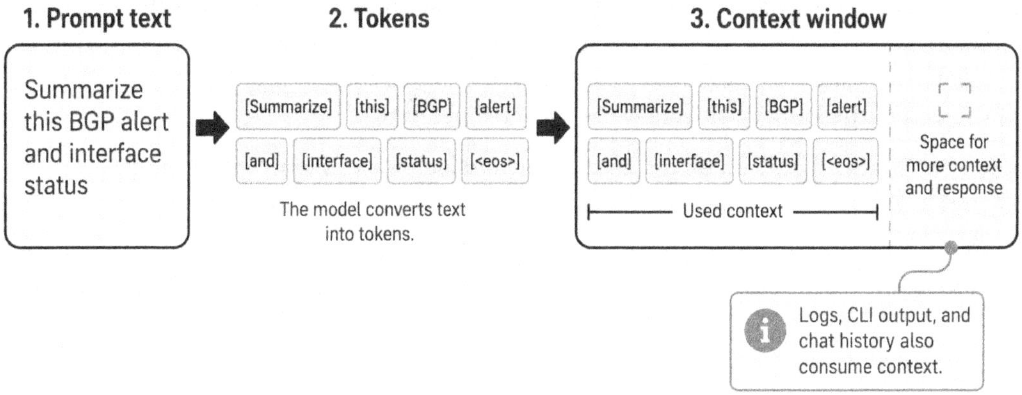

Figure 2.1: How prompt text becomes tokens inside a model context window

For NetOps, the lesson is simple: do not paste everything just because you can. Give the model the right context, not all context. Later, when we build prompt templates and tool outputs, we will keep this in mind by sending focused data instead of dumping every log line into the prompt.

Managing output size and cost

When you run a local model with Ollama, you are not paying per token. That is one reason local development is so useful. You can experiment freely, break things, test prompts, and learn how the model behaves without watching usage charges grow.

That does not mean tokens stop mattering. Large prompts still take more time. Large outputs still consume compute. If you later move the same workflow to a cloud model, tokens can also affect cost. The discipline we build locally still matters when the workflow grows up.

A practical habit is to ask for only what you need. If you need **JavaScript Object Notation (JSON)**, ask for JSON. If you need five fields, do not ask for a long explanation. If the output will feed another tool, keep it structured and small enough for the next step to validate.

That brings us to the first model setting that most engineers notice when they start experimenting: temperature.

Controlling temperature and predictable output

Temperature controls how random or varied the model output can be. Lower temperature makes output more predictable. Higher temperature allows more variation. For creative writing, brainstorming, or naming ideas, variation can be useful. For network automation, variation is usually the thing we are trying to avoid.

If you ask a model to generate a short explanation of **Border Gateway Protocol (BGP)**, a little variation is fine. If you ask it to return a JSON object with specific fields, variation can break the workflow. One extra sentence before the JSON block may be enough to break a parser. That is why structured network tasks usually use a low temperature.

For network tasks, start with predictable output and increase variation only when the use case requires it. *Table 2.2* gives practical starting points for temperature settings:

Use case	Suggested temperature	Why this setting helps
Structured JSON extraction	0.0 to 0.2	Keeps output consistent and easier to validate
Command output parsing	0.0 to 0.3	Reduces drift in field names and structure
Configuration templates	0.0 to 0.3	Makes generated structure more repeatable
Documentation summaries	0.5 to 0.8	Allows more natural wording while staying grounded
Brainstorming ideas	0.8 to 1.2	Encourages variation when exact structure is not required

Table 2.2: Practical temperature settings for network operations tasks

The important part is not memorizing the values. The important part is knowing what you are optimizing for. If the output feeds automation, optimize for consistency. If the output is a human-readable explanation, you have more room for natural language.

Comparing temperature behavior

The repository includes a simple temperature example in `examples/temperature.py`. The file sends a prompt to the local Ollama API and changes the temperature setting so you can see how the output changes.

The core idea looks like this:

```
import requests

prompt = "Generate a BGP configuration for AS 65001 with neighbor 10.0.0.1"

response = requests.post("http://localhost:11434/api/generate", json={
    "model": "llama3.2:3b",
    "prompt": prompt,
    "stream": False,
    "options": {
        "temperature": 1.5,
        "num_predict": 200
    }
}).json()

print(response["response"])
```

Run the example from the root of the repository:

```
python3 examples/temperature.py
```

Your output will not match another reader's output exactly, especially with a higher temperature. That is the point of the lab. Run it a few times, lower the temperature, and compare what changes. You are not just testing the script. You are learning how much control your workflow needs.

Once you see temperature change the output, the next behavior to understand is even more important for agents: the model does not remember previous calls unless your application provides that memory.

Understanding stateless calls and memory

LLM API calls are **stateless** by default. That means one request does not automatically remember what happened in the previous request. If you ask the model *What is BGP?* and then make a separate call asking *What did I just ask you?*, the model will not know unless your application sends the earlier message again.

This surprises a lot of people because chat applications feel like they remember. The application is doing that work. It stores the **conversation history** and sends relevant parts of that history back to the model. The model is not secretly keeping your troubleshooting session open somewhere by itself.

The difference is shown in *Figure 2.2*. A stateless call sends only the current prompt. A memory-enabled application sends the current prompt plus selected conversation history or summarized context:

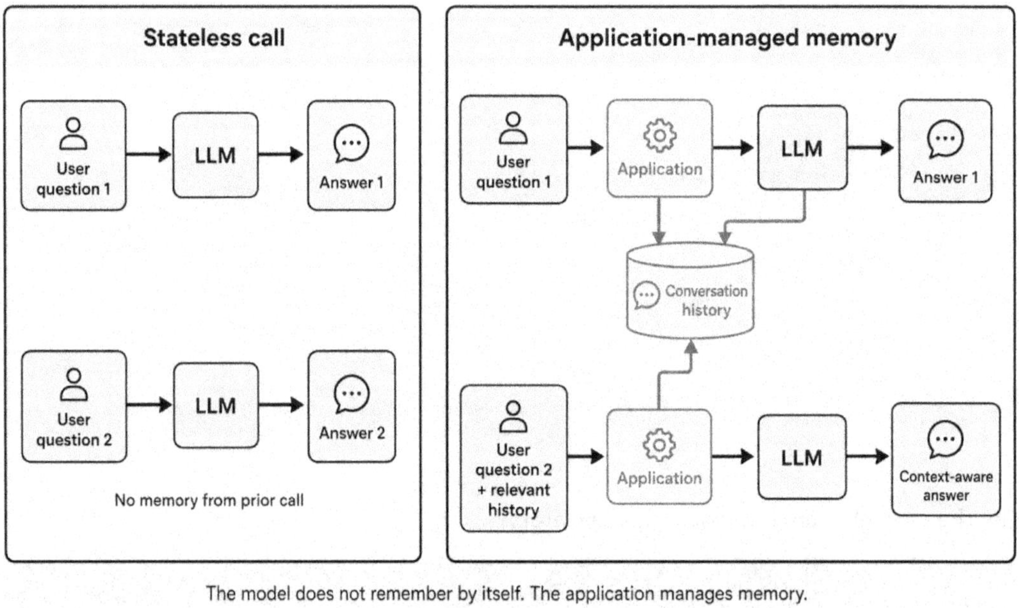

Figure 2.2: Stateless model calls compared with application managed memory

This distinction matters for network agents. Real troubleshooting is rarely one question and one answer. You ask about a neighbor. Then you ask about the interface. Then you ask whether the recent logs explain the state change. If we want the assistant to follow that trail, the application has to manage the history. We will build that pattern later in Chapter 5.

Using Ollama for the local lab

For the hands-on work in this book, we use Ollama as the local model runtime. Ollama lets you download and run models on your own machine. That gives us a safe and cheap place to experiment before we build more complex workflows.

This is especially useful for network engineers because network data can be sensitive. Device names, topology details, configurations, and logs may reveal information you do not want to send to a public service. Local models are not the answer to every production problem, but they are a very good development environment.

The model we will standardize on in this book is `llama3.2:3b`, because it is small enough for most laptops and is already used by the repository. Larger models can produce better results, but they also require more memory and compute. Start small, learn the workflow, and then test larger models when you know what you are measuring.

> **Tip**
>
> If your hardware supports it, you can also try `llama3.1:8b` for comparison. Keep `llama3.2:3b` as the book baseline so your outputs stay close to the repository examples.

We will keep the setup mostly operating system neutral. Sif used a MacBook during the workshop, but Ollama supports macOS, Linux, and Windows. The commands in this chapter are shown from a terminal. Where an operating system needs a special note, we will call that out.

Installing Ollama and pulling the model

The first step is to install Ollama. The exact installer depends on your operating system, but the goal is the same: install Ollama, start the service if needed, and pull the `llama3.2:3b` model.

On macOS, if you use **Homebrew**, the installation can look like this:

```
brew install ollama
ollama pull llama3.2:3b
```

On Linux, the quick installation path can look like this:

```
curl -fsSL https://ollama.com/install.sh | sh
ollama pull llama3.2:3b
```

On Windows, install Ollama from the Windows installer, then open **PowerShell** and pull the model:

```
ollama pull llama3.2:3b
```

After the model is installed, verify that Ollama can see it:

```
ollama list
```

A successful output should look similar to the following. The exact columns may vary by Ollama version, but llama3.2:3b should be visible in the model list:

```
$ ollama list

NAME            ID              SIZE      MODIFIED
llama3.2:3b     a80c4f17acd5    2.0 GB    2 minutes ago
```

Once the model appears in the list, we can test it from the command line before writing any Python. That keeps the setup troubleshooting simple.

Running the model from the command line

The command line test answers a very simple question: can Ollama run the model and return a response? If this fails, do not move on to Python yet. Fix the local model first.

Run the following command:

```
ollama run llama3.2:3b
```

Then try a simple networking prompt:

```
Explain BGP route selection in three bullet points
```

You should receive a short explanation. The wording may differ from what another reader sees, and that is fine. We are checking that the model responds, not that it produces a specific paragraph.

If you prefer a one-shot command, some Ollama versions allow passing the prompt directly after the model name. If your version supports it, this style is useful for quick tests:

```
ollama run llama3.2:3b "Explain BGP route selection in three bullet points"
```

Now that the model responds from the terminal, the next step is to verify that the repository and Python environment can talk to it.

Setting up the repository and Python environment

The repository contains the examples used throughout the book. Clone the Packt repository first, then install the Python packages from requirements.txt:

```
git clone https://github.com/PacktPublishing/Building-AI-Agents-for-Network-
Operations.git
cd Building-AI-Agents-for-Network-Operations
```

```
python3 -m venv .venv
source .venv/bin/activate
pip install -r requirements.txt
```

On Windows PowerShell, activating the **virtual environment** usually looks like this:

```
.venv\Scripts\Activate.ps1
pip install -r requirements.txt
```

The virtual environment keeps this book's dependencies isolated from the rest of your machine. That matters because we will build several scripts over the next few chapters, and we do not want one project's packages to break another project.

With the dependencies installed, run the setup test script from the root of the repository:

```
python3 examples/test_setup.py
```

The script checks the Python version, verifies that Ollama is installed and running, checks for the `llama3.2:3b` model, and confirms that the expected lab files are present. A successful run should look similar to this:

```
$ python3 examples/test_setup.py

🤖 AI Networking Workshop - Setup Test
100% Free with Ollama - No API Keys!

======================================================================
Python Version Check
======================================================================
✅ Python 3.12.3

======================================================================
Ollama Check
======================================================================
✅ Ollama installed
✅ Ollama service running
✅ llama3.2:3b model installed

======================================================================
Lab Files Check
======================================================================
```

```
☑ labs/lab1-ollama/simple_ollama_test.py
☑ labs/lab3-chatbot/chatbot_v2_with_memory.py
☑ labs/lab4-agentic/agentic_network_bot_ollama.py

============================================================================
Summary
============================================================================
☑ All checks passed! You're ready!

Next: python3 labs/lab1-ollama/simple_ollama_test.py
```

If this script passes, your local lab is ready. If it fails, the error message usually points to the missing step, such as Ollama not running or the model not being installed.

Calling Ollama from Python

Now we can move from the command line to Python. This is the first step toward building agents, because our application code needs to send prompts, receive responses, and decide what to do with the result.

The main file for this part of the chapter is `labs/lab1-ollama/simple_ollama_test.py`. It uses the `requests` library to call the local Ollama API at `http://localhost:11434/api/generate`. The core function sends a prompt, sets model options, and returns the response with token counts.

The simplified version looks like this:

```
import requests

def chat_with_ollama(
    prompt,
    model="llama3.2:3b",
    temperature=0.7,
    max_tokens=500
):
    url = "http://localhost:11434/api/generate"
    payload = {
        "model": model,
        "prompt": prompt,
        "stream": False,
        "options": {
            "temperature": temperature,
```

```
            "num_predict": max_tokens
        }
    }

    response = requests.post(url, json=payload, timeout=30)
    response.raise_for_status()
    data = response.json()

    return data["response"]

answer = chat_with_ollama("Explain OSPF in two sentences")
print(answer)
```

This is not a full agent yet. It is just a controlled local model call. But this pattern is the foundation for everything we build later: your code creates the request, sends it to the model, receives the result, and decides what happens next.

Run the full lab file from the repository root:

```
python3 labs/lab1-ollama/simple_ollama_test.py
```

You should see an Ollama test header, a simple response, token counts, and then an interactive prompt. The exact response text will vary, which is expected. What matters is that the script can connect to Ollama and return a response. A successful output should look similar to this:

```
$ python3 labs/lab1-ollama/simple_ollama_test.py

🤖 Ollama API Test - AI Networking Workshop
======================================================================
📝 Test 1: Simple Chat
Response: OSPF is a link state routing protocol used inside an autonomous system.
Tokens: 48

📝 Test 3: Temperature Effects
======================================================================
💬 Interactive Mode - Type quit to exit
======================================================================
```

This small script gives us three important building blocks: an API call, generation options, and response parsing. The `chat_with_ollama()` function is the pattern we will keep reusing in later labs. Get familiar with it now, because it becomes the foundation for chatbots, tool calls, and agents.

Reviewing what the Python code is doing

This script is doing a few important things. First, it builds a JSON payload that tells Ollama which model to use and what prompt to answer. Second, it sends the request to the local Ollama API. Third, it reads the JSON response and extracts the model output.

The `stream` field is set to `False` because we want the complete response returned in one payload. Streaming is useful in chat interfaces, but it adds complexity that we do not need yet.

The `options` block controls generation behavior. In this chapter, the important options are `temperature` and `num_predict`. Temperature controls randomness. `num_predict` limits how many tokens the model generates.

The function also catches connection errors in the full repository version. That matters because local services fail in boring ways. Ollama may not be running. The model may not be downloaded. The port may be unavailable. Good code should tell the reader what failed instead of throwing an unreadable stack trace.

With the basic call working, we can use the same function to explore temperature in a more controlled way.

Experimenting with temperature from Python

The `simple_ollama_test.py` file includes a temperature comparison function. It sends the same prompt with different temperature values so you can see how much the output changes.

The relevant idea looks like this:

```
temperatures = [0.0, 0.7, 1.5]

for temp in temperatures:
    result = chat_with_ollama(
        "Generate a creative name for a network monitoring tool",
        model="llama3.2:3b",
        temperature=temp
    )
    print(f"Temperature {temp}: {result}")
```

For a creative naming task, higher temperature may produce more interesting output. For network parsing, that same variation can become a problem. If we ask for structured output, we usually want predictable field names, predictable nesting, and no extra commentary before or after the result.

Try changing the prompt to something more structured, such as this:

```
Return three BGP neighbor states as a JSON array
```

Then run the script with a lower temperature and a higher temperature. You will start to see why later chapters use strict prompts, schemas, and validation for anything that feeds automation.

Reviewing tokens in the lab

The repository includes `examples/tokens_test.py`, which demonstrates token counting with the Ollama Python package. The exact token count can vary depending on the model and package version, but the lesson is the same: prompts and responses consume tokens, and those tokens affect context size and performance.

A simple example might send a short network configuration snippet to the model and print the prompt token count. The file uses a small BGP configuration as input so the example stays familiar:

```
router bgp 65001
 neighbor 10.0.0.1 remote-as 65002
 neighbor 10.0.0.1 description CORE-RTR-01
```

For now, do not worry about the exact number. The important habit is paying attention to how much data you send. Later, when we pass tool results, command outputs, and conversation history into the model, token discipline becomes part of good agent design.

Troubleshooting and production considerations

The local lab is intentionally simple, but it still gives us a chance to build good habits. When something fails, test the setup one layer at a time before changing the agent code.

Troubleshooting the local setup

Local setup issues are usually simple, but they can be frustrating if you do not know where to look. The best approach is to test one layer at a time: Python, Ollama, the model, the repository, and then the lab script.

Table 2.3 lists common setup issues and what to check first:

Problem	**Likely cause**	**First check**
ollama command not found	Ollama is not installed or not on the path	Reinstall Ollama and open a new terminal
Cannot connect to Ollama	Ollama service is not running	Run `ollama serve` and try again
Model not found	`llama3.2:3b` has not been downloaded	Run `ollama pull llama3.2:3b`
Python import error	Dependencies are missing from the virtual environment	Run `pip install -r requirements.txt`
Lab files missing	Command is being run from the wrong directory	Run commands from the repository root
Response is too slow	Local hardware is limited or model is too large	Use `llama3.2:3b` before testing larger models

Table 2.3: Common local setup issues and first troubleshooting steps

The repository also provides `examples/test_setup.py` for this exact reason. If something feels wrong, run the setup test before debugging the agent code. Start with the boring checks. They save time.

Checking production reality

This chapter uses local models because they are perfect for learning and experimentation. You can iterate quickly, keep data on your machine, and avoid API costs. That does not automatically mean every production system should run on a small local model.

Production choices depend on performance, data sensitivity, governance, latency, and quality requirements. Some teams may use hosted models. Some may run private models on internal infrastructure. Some may use local models for development and stronger models for production. The architecture should let you change that decision without rewriting everything.

That is why our code should keep model calls isolated. If the rest of the system talks to a clean function such as `chat_with_ollama()`, we can later replace the backend with another model provider, a private endpoint, or a larger local model. The rest of the agent does not need to care as much.

The production habit starts here: build small, keep boundaries clean, validate outputs, and make it easy to swap components later.

Summary

In this chapter, we looked at the LLM fundamentals that matter for network operations. We covered tokens, context windows, temperature, stateless API calls, and why memory belongs in the application rather than the model itself.

We also set up Ollama, pulled the `llama3.2:3b` model, verified the environment, ran a local model from the command line, and called it from Python. That gives us the local lab we need for the rest of the book.

The key lesson is simple: LLMs are useful, but they are not magic. They work best when we give them focused context, control their output, and wrap them with code that validates what they return. That is the foundation for every practical agent we will build.

In the next chapter, we will use this foundation to write better prompts for network automation. We will move from asking broad questions to designing prompts that produce consistent, structured, and useful output for real NetOps tasks.

Join us on Discord

For discussions around the book and to connect with your peers, join us on Discord at `packt.link/discordcloud` or scan the QR code below:

3

Prompt Engineering for Network Automation

Most network automation failures do not start with bad intentions. They start with a vague request. Someone asks a model to analyze a config, fix a network issue, or summarize an alert, and the model responds with something that looks useful at first glance. Then the workflow breaks because the output is too chatty, the fields are inconsistent, or the model made a confident guess that was not actually in the data.

That is where prompt engineering becomes practical. We are not trying to write clever sentences for a chatbot. We are trying to give a **large language model (LLM)** enough structure to behave predictably inside a network operations workflow. The prompt becomes part of the system design.

For network work, that means the prompt must tell the model what role it is playing, what examples to follow, what context matters, and what output format the rest of the workflow expects. If the output needs to feed a script, it cannot be a beautiful paragraph. It needs to be structured, constrained, and easy to validate.

In this chapter, we will build that discipline using the **Role, Anchors, Context, and Expected output (RACE) prompt framework**. The goal is simple: turn vague prompts into reusable prompts that produce useful, testable output for network operations.

In this chapter, we will cover the following topics:

- Review the technical requirements for the prompt engineering labs
- Understand why prompt engineering matters for network automation
- Apply the RACE prompt framework to NetOps tasks
- Compare vague prompts with structured prompts

- Build a configuration parser prompt
- Validate model output before using it in workflows
- Create reusable prompt templates for common operations tasks
- Troubleshoot common prompt failures

By the end of this chapter, you will have a practical way to design prompts that can support parsing, triage, documentation, and later agent workflows. That matters because every agent we build later will depend on the quality of the instructions, examples, context, and output rules we give it.

Technical requirements

This chapter builds on the local setup from *Chapter 2*. You should already have **Ollama** installed, the `llama3.2:3b` model pulled locally, and the book repository cloned to your machine.

You will use the following files from the repository:

- `labs/lab2-prompts/prompt_engineering_race.py`
- `labs/lab2-prompts/PROMPT_TEMPLATES.md`
- `labs/lab2-prompts/netmiko_config_parser.py`
- `prompts/bad_prompt.txt`
- `prompts/race_network_analysis_prompt.txt`

The prompt engineering examples use local model calls through Ollama. The network data is mocked by default, so you do not need access to real routers or switches to complete this chapter. If you later want to connect to real devices, the optional `netmiko_config_parser.py` file shows the pattern, but we will keep the main lab read-only and mock-based for now.

From the repository root, you should be able to run the main prompt engineering lab with this command:

```
python3 labs/lab2-prompts/prompt_engineering_race.py
```

If your local repository has not yet been updated to the final RACE file names, use the equivalent Lab 2 prompt engineering file in the same folder. The book uses the RACE naming consistently so the framework and chapter terminology stay aligned.

Understanding why prompt engineering matters

A prompt is not just a question. In an automation workflow, a prompt is an interface between your code, your network data, and the model. If that interface is vague, the output will be vague. If that interface is structured, the model has a much better chance of producing something your workflow can use.

This is especially true in **network operations (NetOps)** because the input data is often messy. **Command line interface (CLI)** output may be vendor-specific. A log message may be incomplete. A ticket may contain user language instead of technical detail. A configuration snippet may be missing the surrounding context. The model can help interpret these inputs, but only if we tell it what to focus on and what not to invent.

Here is a prompt that looks harmless but causes problems quickly:

```
Parse this config and tell me what is wrong.
```

The model may answer with a paragraph, a list, a guessed root cause, or even a sample parser. None of that is automatically wrong for a human conversation, but it is not reliable for automation. If the next step expects **JavaScript Object Notation (JSON)**, this kind of prompt is not enough.

Before we write a single production prompt, we need a framework that makes the model behavior easier to predict. That is where RACE comes in.

Introducing the RACE prompt framework

The RACE framework gives us a simple structure for building prompts that work better in network automation. It is not magic, and it is not a replacement for testing. It is a checklist that helps us avoid the most common prompt mistakes.

The four parts are shown in *Table 3.1*:

RACE element	What it does	Network example
Role	Defines the perspective or expertise the model should use	Act as a network automation engineer reviewing interface output

RACE element	What it does	Network example
Anchors	Gives examples or patterns the model can follow	Provide sample CLI input and the exact JSON output shape
Context	Provides the relevant network facts, constraints, and environment details	Tell the model the output is from Arista EOS and the task is read only
Expected output	Defines the response format, fields, and rules	Return one JSON object only, use null for missing values, and do not explain the answer

Table 3.1: The RACE prompt framework for network automation

The table gives us the structure. The next step is understanding how each part changes model behavior in practice.

Defining the role

The **role** tells the model what kind of perspective to use. For network work, this usually means giving the model a specific operational identity: network automation engineer, senior network engineer, Network Operations Center engineer, security analyst, or documentation assistant.

A weak role sounds like this:

```
You are helpful.
```

A stronger role sounds like this:

```
You are a network automation engineer extracting structured facts from device CLI
output.
```

The second version is not longer for the sake of being longer. It narrows the model's behavior. We are not asking for general helpfulness. We are asking for structured extraction from network data.

Adding anchors

Anchors are examples that show the model what good input and output look like. Examples are often more powerful than instructions alone because they give the model a concrete pattern to follow.

For example, if we want interface output converted to JSON, the prompt should include a short sample input and a matching sample output. That tells the model the field names, the value types, and the structure we expect. It also helps reduce drift between runs.

Anchors matter because smaller local models can be literal in odd ways. If you only describe the output, the model may still format it differently. If you show the output, you give it a pattern.

Providing context

Context is the operational information the model needs to answer correctly. In network automation, context may include the vendor, platform, command, topology, device role, severity, or workflow constraints.

The context should be focused. Do not paste the entire network into the prompt just because the context window allows it. If the task is to parse one interface, give it the interface output and the schema. If the task is to triage one alert, give it the alert, device role, and relevant state. The goal is useful context, not all context.

Defining the expected output

The **expected output** section is where many automation prompts either succeed or fail. If the output feeds a script, define the exact format. If you need JSON, say JSON. If fields can be missing, say whether to use `null`, an empty array, or a specific error object. If you do not want explanations, say that clearly.

A practical expected output section might look like this:

```
EXPECTED OUTPUT:
Return one JSON object only.
Do not use markdown fences.
Do not explain your answer.
Use null for missing values.
Do not invent values that are not present in the input.
```

This is not about being rude to the model. It is about writing instructions that make the output safe for the next step in the workflow.

The complete RACE flow is easier to remember when we see the pieces together. *Figure 3.1* shows how the framework turns a vague request into a structured prompt that a network automation workflow can validate:

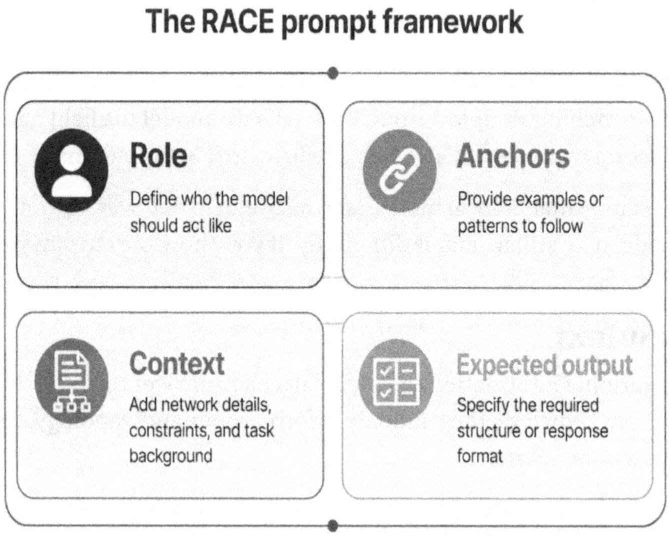

Figure 3.1: RACE prompt framework for network automation

Keep this figure in mind as we move into the lab. Every prompt we write in this chapter will use the same basic pattern: define the role, anchor the behavior, provide the right context, and specify the expected output.

Comparing vague prompts with structured prompts

The fastest way to see why structure matters is to compare a vague prompt with a RACE prompt. The vague prompt may produce something readable. The structured prompt is designed to produce something useful for automation.

The repository includes a weak prompt in `prompts/bad_prompt.txt`. It is intentionally short:

```
Parse this config and tell me what is wrong.
```

This prompt has no role, no examples, no network context, and no expected output format. The model has to guess what the user wants. A human might understand the intent, but an automation workflow cannot depend on guesses.

Table 3.2 compares the vague version with a structured prompt design:

Prompt quality	What the prompt says	Likely result
Vague prompt	Parse this config	Free form explanation, inconsistent fields, possible guesses
Structured RACE prompt	Role, examples, context, JSON schema, and output rules	More consistent JSON that can be parsed and validated

Table 3.2: Comparing vague prompts with structured RACE prompts

That difference matters because we are not only asking the model to be helpful; we are asking it to produce output that another part of the system can consume.

Building a configuration parser prompt

Now let us build the first practical prompt in this chapter: a configuration parser prompt. The goal is to take raw interface output and return structured JSON with fields such as interface name, administrative status, operational status, IP address, prefix length, MAC address, and maximum transmission unit.

The lab file defines a schema that the output must follow. The simplified version of that schema looks like this:

```
INTERFACE_SCHEMA = {
    "type": "object",
    "properties": {
        "interface": {"type": "string"},
        "admin_status": {"type": "string", "enum": ["up", "down"]},
        "oper_status": {"type": "string", "enum": ["up", "down"]},
        "ip_address": {"type": ["string", "null"]},
        "prefix_length": {"type": ["integer", "null"]},
        "mac_address": {"type": ["string", "null"]},
        "mtu": {"type": ["integer", "null"]}
    },
    "required": [
        "interface",
        "admin_status",
        "oper_status",
```

```
            "ip_address",
            "prefix_length",
            "mac_address",
            "mtu"
        ],
        "additionalProperties": False
    }
```

The important part is not memorizing the schema. The important part is that the schema gives the workflow something concrete to validate. If the model returns a missing field, a wrong type, or an unexpected status value, the code can detect that before the result moves downstream.

Writing the RACE prompt

A RACE prompt for this parser needs to do four things. It needs to tell the model its role, show an example, provide the raw interface context, and define the expected JSON output. The shortened version looks like this:

```
You are a JSON extraction engine for network automation data.

ROLE:
Extract facts from network interface CLI output so another automation workflow can
consume the result.

ANCHORS:
Example input:
GigabitEthernet0/1 is up, line protocol is up
  Hardware is iGbE, address is 0000.0c07.ac01
  Internet address is 10.0.0.1/24
  MTU 1500 bytes

Example output:
{
  "interface": "GigabitEthernet0/1",
  "admin_status": "up",
  "oper_status": "up",
  "ip_address": "10.0.0.1",
  "prefix_length": 24,
  "mac_address": "0000.0c07.ac01",
  "mtu": 1500
}
```

```
CONTEXT:
Parse the interface output provided below. Only use facts present in the input.

EXPECTED OUTPUT:
Return one JSON object only.
Do not write Python code.
Do not use markdown fences.
Use null for missing values.
Do not invent values.

NOW PARSE THIS CONFIG:
{config_text}
```

Notice the tone of the prompt. It is not trying to be clever. It is trying to be specific. We are telling the model the job, the pattern, the data, and the output rules. That is the core of prompt engineering for automation.

Running the prompt engineering lab

Run the main lab file from the repository root with the following command:

```
python3 labs/lab2-prompts/prompt_engineering_race.py
```

The script first runs a vague prompt and then runs the structured RACE prompt. A successful run should look similar to this:

```
RACE Prompt Engineering Workshop
======================================================================


Framework:
  R - Role
  A - Anchors
  C - Context
  E - Expected output

Goal:
  Show why vague prompts fail and structured prompts work better
  for network automation use cases.

Config Parser Test
======================================================================
```

```
BAD PROMPT
----------------------------------------------------------------------
Prompt:
Parse this config

LLM Result:
This appears to be interface output...

GOOD PROMPT USING RACE
----------------------------------------------------------------------
Prompt length: 2100 characters

LLM Result:
{
  "interface": "GigabitEthernet0/2",
  "admin_status": "down",
  "oper_status": "down",
  "ip_address": null,
  "prefix_length": null,
  "mac_address": "0000.0c07.ac02",
  "mtu": 1500
}

Evaluation
----------------------------------------------------------------------
Valid JSON detected.
JSON passed schema validation.
```

Your exact wording may differ because local model output can vary. The important part is that the RACE prompt produces structured JSON that can be parsed and validated.

Reviewing what the lab is doing

The lab has three pieces worth paying attention to. First, it builds a prompt. Second, it calls the local Ollama API. Third, it extracts and validates the JSON result.

The simplified model call looks like this:

```
def call_llm(prompt, model="llama3.2:3b", temperature=0.0, timeout=60):
    payload = {
        "model": model,
```

```
            "prompt": prompt,
            "stream": False,
            "options": {
                "temperature": temperature
            }
        }

        response = requests.post(
            "http://localhost:11434/api/generate",
            json=payload,
            timeout=timeout
        )
        response.raise_for_status()
        return response.json().get("response", "").strip()
```

The low temperature matters here. We are not asking for creative writing. We are asking for structured extraction. That means predictable output is more valuable than variety.

Validating model output

A prompt can reduce risk, but it cannot eliminate risk. That is why validation belongs in the workflow. If the output will feed another script, dashboard, ticket, or agent step, the code should verify that the structure is usable before trusting it.

The lab uses a JSON extraction helper and a validation function. The simplified validation idea looks like this:

```
parsed = extract_json(good_result)

if parsed is None:
    print("Could not parse the LLM response as JSON")
    return

errors = validate_interface_json(parsed)

if errors:
    print("JSON parsed, but validation found issues")
else:
    print("JSON passed schema validation")
```

This is where the lab becomes more than a prompt demo. It shows the pattern we will keep using later: prompt the model, parse the result, validate the output, and only then let the workflow continue.

A useful way to think about prompt design is as a loop, not a one-time activity. *Figure 3.2* shows the refinement cycle we will use throughout the book:

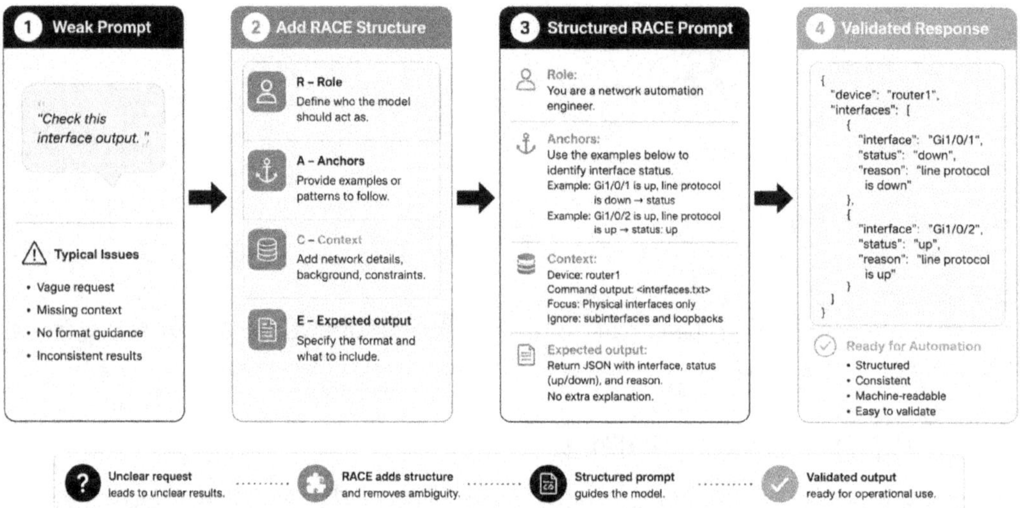

Figure 3.2: Prompt testing and refinement loop

The loop is simple on purpose. Start with a real input, define the expected output, test the prompt, inspect the failure, and refine. That process is slower than copying a prompt from a blog post, but it is much safer for operational workflows.

Creating reusable prompt templates

Once a prompt works, do not leave it buried inside a notebook or chat history. Treat it like code. Save it, version it, test it, and reuse it. The repository includes `labs/lab2-prompts/PROMPT_TEMPLATES.md` as a starting point for a small prompt library.

The template library includes three useful patterns:

- A configuration parser that turns device output into structured JSON
- An alert triage prompt that classifies severity and recommends next steps
- A configuration change risk prompt that scores risk and explains why

Those patterns map nicely to real operations work. They are also the kinds of prompts that can later become tools inside an agent workflow.

Creating an alert triage prompt

Alert triage is a good example because the input is usually incomplete. The prompt needs to classify the alert, explain the reason, and suggest a few practical next steps without pretending to know facts it does not have.

A RACE style alert triage prompt might look like this:

```
ROLE:
You are a Network Operations Center analyst triaging network alerts.

ANCHORS:
Severity must be one of: critical, high, medium, low, false_positive.
Next actions must be specific and operational.

CONTEXT:
Use only the alert text and provided device context.
Do not invent business impact.

EXPECTED OUTPUT:
Return JSON with severity, reason, next_actions, and escalate.
Use two to five next actions.

TRIAGE THIS ALERT:
{alert_text}
```

This prompt is not trying to close the incident. It is trying to produce a cleaner starting point for the engineer. That is a realistic and useful early agent capability.

Creating a documentation prompt

Documentation prompts work best when the input is already somewhat structured. Topology data, device inventory, command output, and incident notes can become useful summaries if the prompt gives the model a clear target.

For example, a documentation prompt might ask the model to produce an overview, list the devices, summarize VLANs or routing relationships, and include a troubleshooting note. The output can still be reviewed by a human, but the first draft becomes much faster.

The key is to keep the prompt grounded in the data. If the topology does not include a second spine switch, the model should not invent one because the design usually has two spines. That is why constraints matter.

Handling common prompt failures

Prompts fail in predictable ways. Once you recognize the pattern, the fix becomes easier. Most failures come from missing context, weak examples, unclear output rules, or expecting the model to infer too much.

Table 3.3 lists common prompt failures and practical fixes:

Failure mode	What it looks like	Practical fix
Output is too chatty	The model explains before returning data	Add an expected output rule such as return JSON only
Field names drift	The model returns `interface_name` in one run and intf in another	Provide a schema and example output
Values are invented	The model fills missing data with a plausible value	Tell the model to use null for missing values and do not invent facts
Wrong device context	The model gives Cisco syntax for Arista output	State the vendor and platform in the context
Prompt works once but not reliably	The same prompt gives different structures across runs	Lower temperature and add anchors

Table 3.3: Common prompt failures and practical fixes

None of these failures mean the model is useless. They mean the prompt and the surrounding workflow need more structure. This is engineering work, not magic.

Extending prompts to live device data

So far, the chapter has focused on mock data. That is the right place to start. Mock data makes the lab safe and repeatable. The optional `netmiko_config_parser.py` file shows how the same prompt pattern can be applied to data collected through **Secure Shell (SSH)** using **Netmiko**.

The file uses a `USE_MOCK` flag so you can switch between mock data and live device access. The default should stay safe:

```
USE_MOCK = True
```

When `USE_MOCK` is set to `True`, the script returns realistic interface configuration snippets from the local mock data. When set to `False`, the script can use Netmiko to connect to devices defined in `DEVICE_CONFIG`. That is useful later, but do not point this at production devices while you are learning.

This pattern is important because it separates prompt design from data collection. The prompt does not need to know whether the data came from a mock dictionary, a file, or a real switch. It only needs clean input and clear output rules.

Checking production reality

Prompt engineering for production is less about finding a perfect prompt and more about building a prompt that behaves well inside a system. That means prompts need version control, tests, validation, and operational boundaries.

A production-ready prompt should answer a few basic questions:

- What role is the model expected to take?
- What examples anchor the expected pattern?
- What context is required and what context should be excluded?
- What format must the output use?
- How will the output be validated?
- What should happen when validation fails?

If you cannot answer those questions, the prompt is not ready for automation. It may still be useful in a chat window, but that is a different risk profile.

The safest habit is to treat prompts like software assets. Keep them in files, review changes, test edge cases, and avoid silently changing prompts in production workflows. A small prompt edit can change system behavior just like a small code edit can.

Summary

In this chapter, we moved from casual prompting to structured prompt design. The main idea is simple: vague prompts produce vague behavior, and automation needs predictable output.

We introduced the **Role, Anchors, Context, and Expected output (RACE)** prompt framework and used it to build prompts for configuration parsing, alert triage, documentation, and validation. We also looked at how prompt failures show up and how to fix them with better roles, examples, context, constraints, output formats, and validation.

The most important habit is to treat prompts as part of the system. Write them carefully. Test them with messy data. Validate their outputs. Keep them versioned. Do not assume a good-looking answer is safe to automate.

In the next chapter, we will take these ideas and apply them to raw network output. We will parse interface state, BGP neighbor summaries, and multi-vendor command outputs into structured data that later agents can use.

Get this book's PDF version and more

Scan the QR code (or go to `packtpub.com/unlock`). Search for this book by name, confirm the edition, and then follow the steps on the page.

UNLOCK NOW

Note: Keep your invoice handy. Purchases made directly from Packt don't require an invoice.

4

Parsing Network Outputs into Structured Data

Network engineers spend a lot of time looking at text. Device output, logs, alerts, configuration snippets, routing tables, and ticket notes are all text in some form. Humans can read that text and make sense of it, but automation needs something more predictable.

That is where **structured data** comes in. If we can turn raw **command line interface (CLI)** output into **JavaScript Object Notation (JSON)**, we can validate it, filter it, pass it to another script, store it, or hand it to an agent as clean context. The model can help with that conversion, but only if we make the output testable.

This chapter takes the prompt engineering discipline from Chapter 3 and applies it to real network-style outputs. We will parse interface status, **Border Gateway Protocol (BGP)** summaries, and multi-vendor examples. We will also look at failure handling because the first rule of operational automation is simple: bad input happens.

By the end of this chapter, you will understand how to move from messy network text to structured data that later chatbots, tools, and agents can use safely. The goal is not to pretend that a **large language model (LLM)** is a perfect parser. The goal is to build a practical parsing workflow with validation and recovery built in.

In this chapter, we will cover the following topics:

- Review the technical requirements and parse lab files
- Understand why structured output matters for network automation
- Move from raw CLI text to validated JSON
- Parse interface output into structured fields
- Parse BGP summary output for neighbor state

- Normalize multi-vendor interface outputs
- Handle malformed output and parsing failures
- Decide when to use LLM-assisted parsing or deterministic parsing

These topics give us the bridge between better prompts and useful agents. Before an agent can reason over network state, the state has to be represented in a form the rest of the application can trust.

Technical requirements

Before running the examples in this chapter, make sure your local lab from Chapter 2 is working. You should be able to run `Ollama`, use the `llama3.2:3b` model, and execute Python scripts from the root of the repository.

This chapter uses the following files from the repository:

- `labs/lab1-ollama/json_output_challenge.py`
- `labs/lab1-ollama/challenge_1_interface_parser.py`
- `labs/lab1-ollama/challenge_2_bgp_parser.py`
- `labs/lab1-ollama/challenge_3_multi_vendor.py`
- `labs/lab1-ollama/challenge_4_error_handling.py`
- `labs/lab2-prompts/netmiko_config_parser.py`
- `examples/interface_output.json`
- `examples/bgp_output.json`

The examples use mock data by default, so you do not need access to a live router or switch. The `Netmiko` example later in the chapter shows how the same pattern can be connected to live devices, but we will keep that path read-only and optional.

Understanding why structured output matters for NetOps

A human can look at a wall of CLI output and still make progress. We can visually scan for an interface name, spot an `Idle` BGP neighbor, or notice that a field is missing. Code is less forgiving. If the output shifts by one column, a brittle parser can break. If the model returns a paragraph instead of JSON, the next workflow step may fail.

For **network operations (NetOps)** work, structured output gives us a contract. Instead of asking the model to tell us what it thinks, we ask it to return specific fields in a specific format.

That is the difference between a useful assistant and a workflow that falls apart when it sees a slightly different prompt.

Before writing a parser, it helps to decide which fields we actually need. *Table 4.1* shows common network outputs and examples of useful fields to extract:

Network output	**Useful structured fields**	**Why it matters**
Interface status	`interface`, `admin_status`, `oper_status`, `ip_address`, `mtu`	Supports link checks, alert enrichment, and inventory updates
BGP summary	`router_id`, `local_as`, `neighbor`, `state`, `prefixes_received`	Helps identify failed peers and empty route advertisements
Interface errors	`input_errors`, `crc_errors`, `drops`, `last_change`	Supports physical layer and congestion troubleshooting
Device inventory	`hostname`, `model`, `version`, `serial_number`	Supports asset tracking and change planning
Log entries	`timestamp`, `device`, `severity`, `message`, `event_type`	Supports timeline building and incident summaries

Table 4.1: Common network outputs and useful structured fields

The important point is not that every workflow needs the same fields. The important point is that each workflow should know what it expects before the model responds. That expectation is what lets us validate the output instead of just hoping it looks right.

Moving from raw CLI text to validated JSON

The parsing pattern we will use in this chapter is simple: start with raw network text, ask the model for a strict JSON shape, parse the model response, validate the fields, and only then pass the result to the next step. The model helps with the text transformation. The application owns the validation.

The pipeline in *Figure 4.1* shows the flow we will use throughout the chapter:

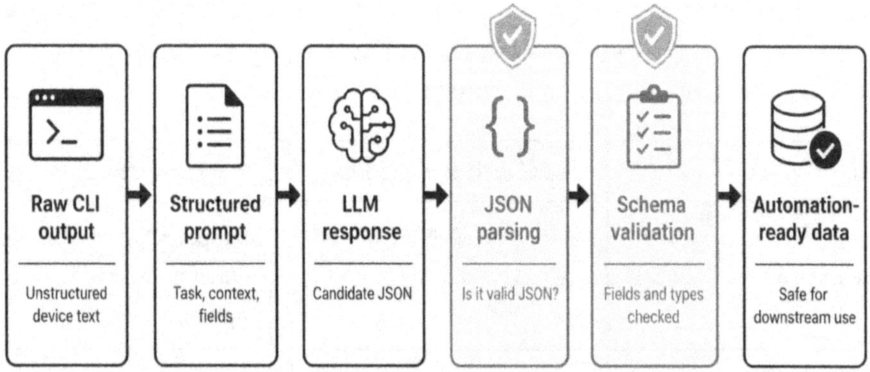

Figure 4.1: From raw CLI output to validated JSON

This flow is useful because it separates the model output from application trust. The model can suggest structure, but the code decides whether that structure is valid enough to use. Before a parsed result moves forward, the application should check that required fields are present, data types are correct, allowed values make sense, and unsupported or missing values are handled safely. This is why the LLM response should be treated as a candidate result, not trusted data.

The repository scripts use a helper function that wraps each prompt with JSON-only instructions, sends the request to the local **Ollama application programming interface (API)**, and then attempts to parse the response with Python. The core pattern looks like this:

```
def ask_ollama(prompt: str, model: str = "llama3.2:3b")-> dict | None:
    json_prompt = f"""You are a JSON-only API. Return ONLY valid JSON.
No markdown, no explanation, no code fences - just the JSON object.

{prompt}

Output only valid JSON:"""

    response = requests.post(
        "http://localhost:11434/api/generate",
        json={
            "model": model,
            "prompt": json_prompt,
            "stream": False,
            "options": {"temperature": 0.1},
        },
```

```
        timeout=30,
    )
    raw = response.json().get("response", "").strip()
    return json.loads(raw)
```

The low temperature setting matters here. We are not asking for creativity. We want a predictable structure that the next line of code can parse. This same helper pattern appears in the interface, BGP, multi-vendor, and error-handling challenges.

Parsing interface output

Interface output is a good first parsing target because the structure is familiar but still messy enough to be interesting. The output contains useful data, but it is not already in a form that a later workflow can easily consume.

The first lab file is `labs/lab1-ollama/challenge_1_interface_parser.py`. It uses a short Cisco-style interface output and asks the model to return a JSON object with specific fields. Run it from the repository root:

```
python3 labs/lab1-ollama/challenge_1_interface_parser.py
```

A successful run should look similar to the following output:

```
============================================================
Challenge 1: Interface Parser
============================================================

Input (raw CLI output):
GigabitEthernet0/1 is up, line protocol is up
  Hardware is iGbE, address is 0000.0c07.ac01
  Internet address is 10.0.0.1/24
  MTU 1500 bytes, BW 1000000 Kbit/sec

Asking Ollama to parse it...

✅ Parsed JSON:
{
  "interface": "GigabitEthernet0/1",
  "admin_status": "up",
  "oper_status": "up",
  "ip_address": "10.0.0.1",
```

```
  "subnet_mask": null,
  "mac_address": "0000.0c07.ac01",
  "mtu": 1500
}

☑ All expected fields present!
```

Your exact output may vary slightly because the model generates text, but the structure should match the requested fields. If the script returns invalid JSON, that is not a failure of the lesson. It is the lesson. Structured output must always be checked before the rest of the workflow trusts it.

Reviewing the interface prompt

The prompt does two important things. First, it tells the model what kind of output it is parsing. Second, it defines the exact fields that should come back. The important part looks like this:

```
Return a JSON object with exactly these fields:
- interface: string
- admin_status: "up" or "down"
- oper_status: "up" or "down"
- ip_address: string or null
- subnet_mask: string or null
- mac_address: string
- mtu: integer
```

That field list is doing more than documentation. It gives the model a target shape. It also gives the code something to validate. Without this structure, the model might produce a summary that is helpful to a human but useless to an automation workflow.

Parsing BGP summary output

The interface example gives us one object. BGP summary output is more interesting because it usually contains a list of peers, and each peer has state that may need follow-up. This is where JSON becomes useful quickly.

The lab file `labs/lab1-ollama/challenge_2_bgp_parser.py` parses a BGP summary into a router object with a list of neighbors. Run it from the repository root:

```
python3 labs/lab1-ollama/challenge_2_bgp_parser.py
```

The output should include a parsed JSON object and a small follow-up check for non-established sessions:

```
============================================================
Challenge 2: BGP Summary Parser
============================================================

☑ Parsed JSON:
{
  "router_id": "10.0.0.11",
  "local_as": 65001,
  "neighbors": [
    {
      "ip": "10.1.1.1",
      "remote_as": 65011,
      "state": "Established",
      "uptime": "3d02h",
      "prefixes_received": 150
    },
    {
      "ip": "10.1.2.0",
      "remote_as": 65013,
      "state": "Idle",
      "uptime": "0:00:00",
      "prefixes_received": 0
    }
  ]
}

📊 Total neighbors: 2
⚠ Non-established sessions:
   10.1.2.0 - Idle
```

The valuable part is not just that the model returned JSON. The valuable part is that the script can now loop over `neighbors`, filter by `state`, and report sessions that need attention. That is the shift from text output to automation-ready data.

The filter logic is intentionally simple:

```
neighbors = result.get("neighbors", [])
down = [n for n in neighbors if n.get("state") != "Established"]
```

This is the reason structured output matters. Once the response is parsed into a Python object, normal code can do the boring deterministic work. The LLM handles the messy text conversion. Python handles the filtering.

Normalizing multi-vendor output

Real networks are rarely as clean as a single vendor and a single output format. One device may say `GigabitEthernet0/1 is up, line protocol is up`. Another may use `Ethernet1`. Another may use `ge-0/0/1.0 up up`. The operational meaning may be similar, but the text format is different.

The lab file `labs/lab1-ollama/challenge_3_multi_vendor.py` shows how one prompt template can normalize interface status lines from Cisco, Arista, and Juniper-style outputs into the same JSON shape. Run it from the repository root:

```
python3 labs/lab1-ollama/challenge_3_multi_vendor.py
```

A successful run should produce a normalized view of the vendor outputs:

```
============================================================
Challenge 3: Multi-Vendor Parser
============================================================

Goal: same JSON shape from three different CLI formats

-- Cisco IOS --
   Input:  GigabitEthernet0/1 is up, line protocol is up
   Output: {"vendor": "Cisco IOS", "interface": "GigabitEthernet0/1",
"admin_status": "up", "oper_status": "up"}

-- Arista EOS --
   Input:  Ethernet1 is up, line protocol is up (connected)
   Output: {"vendor": "Arista EOS", "interface": "Ethernet1", "admin_status":
"up", "oper_status": "up"}

-- Juniper JunOS --
   Input:  ge-0/0/1.0             up    up
   Output: {"vendor": "Juniper JunOS", "interface": "ge-0/0/1.0", "admin_status":
"up", "oper_status": "up"}

============================================================
```

```
Normalised results (same shape, any vendor):
Vendor           Interface             Admin    Oper
------------------------------------------------------------
Cisco IOS        GigabitEthernet0/1     up       up
Arista EOS       Ethernet1              up       up
Juniper JunOS    ge-0/0/1.0             up       up
```

This example shows why LLM-assisted parsing can be useful. We are not writing three separate parsers. We are asking the model to map different vendor text into the same operational shape, then using code to inspect the result.

Validating structured output before using it

Getting JSON back is not the finish line. It is only the first gate. The next gate is validation. Valid JSON can still be wrong JSON. It can be missing fields, use the wrong data type, or invent a value that was not present in the source output.

At minimum, a parser should check that required keys exist before downstream code uses the result. The interface challenge includes a simple version of that idea:

```
expected = ["interface", "admin_status", "oper_status", "ip_address", "mtu"]
missing = [field for field in expected if field not in result]

if missing:
    print(f"Missing fields: {missing}")
else:
    print("All expected fields present!")
```

This is not a full schema validator, but it teaches the right instinct. Never assume the model returned what you requested. Check the shape before you treat the data as trustworthy.

In production, this validation should become stricter. You may use a schema library, typed data model, or deterministic checks that confirm values are allowed. In Python, **Pydantic** is a popular option for this because it lets you define typed models and validate incoming data before the rest of the application uses it. For example, `admin_status` should be `up`, `down`, or maybe `unknown`. It should not be a sentence.

Handling malformed output and uncertain states

Real data is messy, and model output can be messy too. A device may return an error state. The model may wrap JSON inside markdown fences. It may add a helpful sentence before the object. It may return an object that parses but does not mean what you expected.

The lab file `labs/lab1-ollama/challenge_4_error_handling.py` adds recovery logic and better failure behavior. It demonstrates two important ideas: clean up common model formatting mistakes and return a useful error instead of crashing.

The recovery flow is shown in *Figure 4.2*:

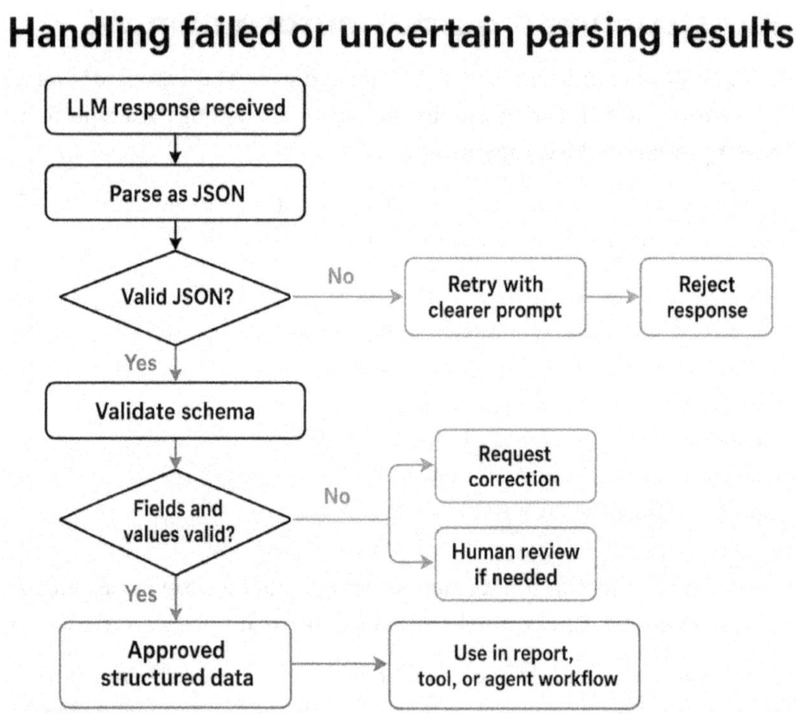

Figure 4.2: Handling failed or uncertain parsing

This flow keeps the parser from pretending every response is safe. If the output can be recovered, the script parses it. If it cannot, the script returns an error message and lets the caller decide what to do next.

Run the error-handling challenge from the repository root:

```
python3 labs/lab1-ollama/challenge_4_error_handling.py
```

A successful run should look similar to this:

```
============================================================
Challenge 4: Error Handling & Graceful Recovery
============================================================

-- Error-disabled port --
   Input: GigabitEthernet0/1 is up, line protocol is down (err-disabled)
   ☑ {"interface": "GigabitEthernet0/1", "admin_status": "up", "oper_status":
"err-disabled", "error_reason": "port-security violation", "warning": null}

-- Flapping / unknown --
   Input: GigabitEthernet0/2 is up, line protocol is unknown
   ☑ {"interface": "GigabitEthernet0/2", "admin_status": "up", "oper_status":
"unknown", "error_reason": null, "warning": "Last flap 00:00:03 ago"}

-- No data available --
   Input: % No interface information available
   ☑ {"interface": null, "admin_status": "unknown", "oper_status": "unknown",
"error_reason": null, "warning": "No interface information available"}

============================================================
Key patterns used in ask_ollama():
  1. Strip markdown fences (``` blocks)
  2. Grab first {...} block if model adds preamble text
  3. Return (result, error) tuple - never raise, never crash
  4. Caller decides what to do with a failure
```

The exact JSON may vary, but the behavior should not. The script should either return structured data or return a controlled error. It should not fail silently, and it should not crash the whole workflow.

Table 4.2 summarizes the failure modes we want to handle as the parsing logic gets more important:

Failure mode	What it looks like	Safeguard
Invalid JSON	Extra prose, markdown fences, or broken braces	Strip common wrappers and retry parsing
Missing fields	No `ip_address`, `state`, or `interface` key	Check required keys before using output
Wrong data type	`mtu` returned as text instead of integer	Validate field types
Hallucinated value	Model invents an `interface` or `state`	Compare against source data where possible
Ambiguous device output	Unknown, empty, or error output	Represent uncertainty explicitly
Timeout or service error	Ollama or network call fails	Return a controlled error and continue

Table 4.2: Parsing failure modes and safeguards

This is where engineering discipline matters. The model may be flexible, but the workflow around it should be boring, predictable, and easy to troubleshoot.

Connecting parsing to live device data carefully

So far, the examples use mock strings inside the scripts. That is intentional. Mock data makes the labs safe and repeatable. At some point, though, a real workflow needs to collect output from a real device or a realistic lab device.

The file `labs/lab2-prompts/netmiko_config_parser.py` shows the next step. It can use mock data by default, or it can fetch output over **Secure Shell (SSH)** with `Netmiko` when you change the configuration. The important safety flag is shown here:

```
USE_MOCK = True  # Flip to False with real devices after the workshop
```

With `USE_MOCK = True`, the script returns built-in interface configuration and status data. With `USE_MOCK = False`, it attempts to connect to devices defined in `DEVICE_CONFIG`. That is useful, but it should stay read only while you are learning.

The production habit is the same as before: start with safe observation. Let the tool collect data. Let the model structure it. Let the code validate it. Do not connect write actions until you have a review and approval workflow around them.

Choosing between LLM-assisted and deterministic parsing

This chapter is about using an LLM to help parse network text, but that does not mean every parsing problem belongs to an LLM. Sometimes a deterministic parser is the better tool. If your device already returns structured JSON, use that. If a mature TextFSM template exists and works reliably, use it. If the format never changes, a simple parser may be enough.

LLM-assisted parsing becomes more attractive when the input is inconsistent, vendor-specific, semi-structured, or mixed with natural language. The model is useful when flexibility matters. Deterministic code is useful when exactness matters.

Table 4.3 gives a practical way to choose between the two approaches:

Situation	**Better starting point**	**Why**
Device returns native JSON	Deterministic parsing	The data is already structured
Known output with stable format	`TextFSM`, `regex`, or custom parser	Predictable text should be parsed predictably
Different vendors return similar meaning in different formats	LLM-assisted parsing with validation	The model can normalize inconsistent text
Incident notes, tickets, or mixed log text	LLM-assisted extraction	The input includes natural language and context

Situation	Better starting point	Why
Compliance or safety-critical decision	Deterministic validation plus human review	The workflow needs auditability and high confidence

Table 4.3: Choosing between deterministic parsing and LLM-assisted parsing

This is not an either-or decision. The best systems often combine both approaches. Use the LLM to handle messy language. Use deterministic code to validate, filter, compare, and decide whether the data is safe to use.

Checking production reality

Parsing is one of those places where demos can look easier than production. A demo usually has clean input and a happy path. A real network has partial output, timeouts, command errors, old device versions, access problems, and vendor differences that were never documented.

For production-style workflows, treat LLM output as untrusted until validated. Store the raw input, the prompt, the raw model response, the parsed result, and the validation outcome. If something breaks at 3 AM, you want to know whether the device returned bad data, the model returned bad JSON, or the application accepted something it should have rejected.

Here are the habits to carry forward:

- Keep raw input for troubleshooting and auditability
- Ask for the smallest useful JSON shape
- Validate required keys and allowed values
- Represent unknown values explicitly instead of guessing
- Fail closed when parsing or validation fails
- Log model responses before and after cleanup
- Use deterministic checks wherever the decision must be exact

These habits are not extra polish. They are what make the difference between a clever parsing demo and a workflow another engineer can trust.

Summary

In this chapter, we turned raw network text into structured data. We used interface output, BGP summaries, multi-vendor interface lines, and error scenarios to show how an LLM can help transform messy CLI output into JSON.

We also kept the important boundary clear. The model can help with text understanding, but the application must validate the result. Valid JSON is not automatically correct JSON. The workflow still needs field checks, type checks, error handling, and logging.

This chapter also showed why read-only parsing is such a good early use case for network agents. It gives us useful operational value while keeping the risk low. We can collect state, normalize data, and prepare context for later workflows without giving the model permission to change anything.

In the next chapter, we will build on this structured data foundation and create a chatbot that can maintain troubleshooting context across multiple questions. That is where the assistant starts to feel less like a one-shot prompt and more like a useful operational helper.

Join us on Discord

For discussions around the book and to connect with your peers, join us on Discord at `packt.link/discordcloud` or scan the QR code below:

5

Building a Network Chatbot with Memory

A chatbot that forgets everything after one question is not very useful during troubleshooting. Network issues rarely arrive as clean, one-question, one-answer problems. They arrive as a trail of clues: an alert, a device name, a neighbor address, an interface state, a log entry, and then one more question after that.

That is where **memory** starts to matter. Not memory in the science fiction sense, and not some magical feature hidden inside the model. For the kind of systems we are building, memory is an application pattern. Your code decides what to keep, what to send back to the model, and what to ignore.

In *Chapter 2*, we saw that **large language model (LLM)** calls are stateless by default. In this chapter, we turn that idea into working Python code. We will first run a chatbot that has no memory, then build a **memory enabled chatbot** that keeps conversation history and uses it to answer follow-up questions.

This chapter is still intentionally local and safe. We are not giving the chatbot live network access yet. The goal is to understand how a conversation becomes stateful before we later connect tools, mock devices, and agent workflows.

In this chapter, we will cover the following topics:

- Reviewing the technical requirements for the chatbot labs
- Understanding why stateless chatbots fail during troubleshooting
- Running a stateless chatbot with Ollama
- Adding application-managed memory with conversation history
- Building the `Network Chatbot` class

- Managing prompts, history, reset, and interactive mode
- Controlling context growth before it becomes a problem
- Preparing chatbot memory for tool calling and agents

By the end of this chapter, you will have a local network assistant that remembers the conversation context. That may not sound flashy, but it is one of the most important steps between a simple prompt and a useful agent.

Technical requirements

This chapter uses the local environment configured in *Chapter 2*. You should have Ollama running locally and the `llama3.2:3b` model installed before starting the labs.

You will use the following files from the repository:

- `labs/lab3-chatbot/chatbot_v1_stateless.py`
- `labs/lab3-chatbot/chatbot_v2_with_memory.py`
- `labs/lab3-chatbot/stateless.MD`
- `labs/lab3-chatbot/memory.MD`

You will also use the `requests` package to call the local Ollama application programming interface (API). If you followed the setup in *Chapter 2*, the dependency should already be installed through `requirements.txt`.

> Tip
>
> The repository also contains `chatbot_v3_live_ssh.py` and `live_ssh.MD`. We will keep live **Secure Shell** (**SSH**) access outside the main flow of this chapter. It is better treated as an optional advanced path after the setup, safety assumptions, and expected output are clear.

With the requirements clear, we can start with the version of the chatbot that intentionally fails. That failure is useful because it shows exactly what memory has to solve.

Understanding why chatbot memory matters

A basic chatbot can answer a single question. That is useful, but it is not how troubleshooting usually works. When you investigate a network issue, each question builds on the last one. You ask about a protocol, then a neighbor, then a device, then a log message, and the meaning of each follow-up depends on the previous context.

A stateless chatbot does not carry that context forward. Every call to the model is independent. If the first request asks about **Open Shortest Path First (OSPF)** and the second request asks what you just asked, the model only sees the second request unless the application sends the first one again.

That is why memory belongs in the application. The application keeps a **conversation history**, builds a prompt that includes relevant previous messages, sends that prompt to the model, and then stores the model response for the next turn.

Figure 5.1 shows the difference between a chatbot that sends each message by itself and a chatbot that sends the current message with selected conversation history:

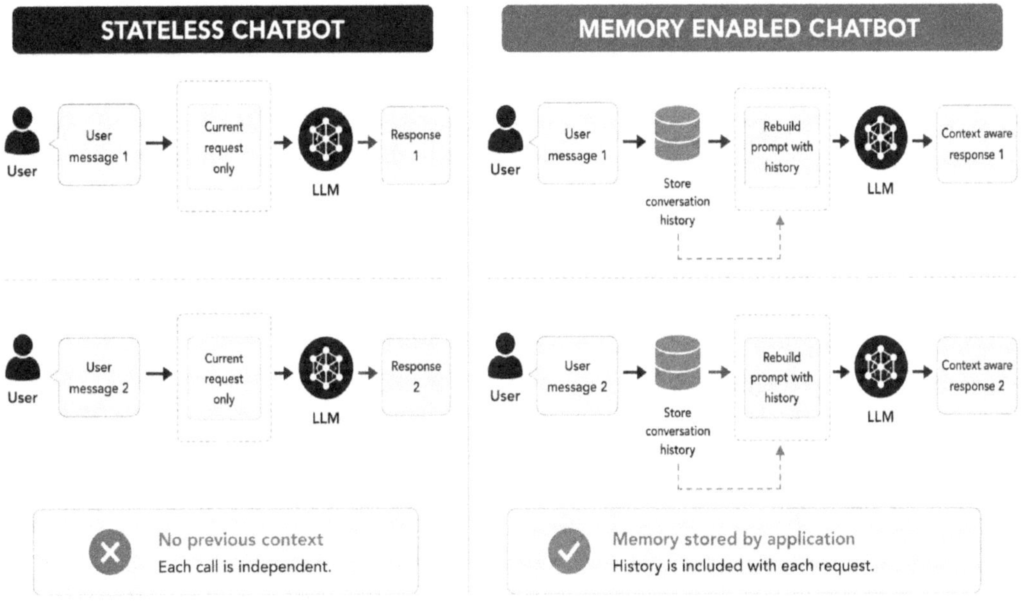

Figure 5.1: Stateless chatbot calls compared with application managed memory

The key difference is where the previous context lives. In the stateless flow, the model receives only the current request, so each turn stands alone. In the memory-enabled flow, the application stores selected conversation history and includes it when building the next prompt, which lets the assistant answer follow-up questions with the earlier troubleshooting context in view.

The pattern in *Figure 5.1* is simple, but it changes what the assistant can do. Once the application carries context forward, the user can ask follow-up questions that depend on earlier messages. That is the behavior we need before we build troubleshooting assistants and agents.

Running a stateless chatbot

The first script, chatbot_v1_stateless.py, demonstrates the problem. It defines a function called simple_chat() that sends a single user message to Ollama. It does not include conversation history.

The key part of the script looks like this:

```
def simple_chat(user_message: str, model: str = "llama3.2:3b")-> str:
    """Send single message with NO conversation history."""
    url = "http://localhost:11434/api/generate"

    payload = {
        "model": model,
        "prompt": user_message,
        "stream": False,
        "options": {
            "temperature": 0.7
        }
    }

    response = requests.post(url, json=payload, timeout=30)
    response.raise_for_status()
    data = response.json()
    return data.get("response", "")
```

The important line is the prompt field. It contains only the current user message. There is no previous question, no assistant response, and no session context.

Run the script from the repository root:

```
python3 labs/lab3-chatbot/chatbot_v1_stateless.py
```

A successful run should look similar to this. The exact model response can vary, but the failure pattern should be the same:

```
🤖 Stateless Chatbot Demo (Ollama)
======================================================================

👤 User: What is OSPF?
🤖 Bot: OSPF is a link-state routing protocol...
```

```
👤 User: What did I just ask you?
🤖 Bot: I do not have access to previous messages...

❌ FAILURE: The bot doesn't remember!
   Each API call is independent.

💡 Next: See chatbot_v2_with_memory.py for the solution!
```

The bot is not broken. It is behaving exactly like the code tells it to behave. The second call does not include the first message, so the model cannot know what came before.

That gives us a clean next step: keep the same local model call, but change what the application sends.

Adding application-managed memory

The second script, `chatbot_v2_with_memory.py`, fixes the problem by storing messages in a list. That list becomes the application memory for the conversation.

The important idea is not complicated. When the user sends a message, the application adds it to history. After the model responds, the application adds the assistant's response to history. On the next turn, the application builds a prompt using the whole history.

The message history uses a simple role and content shape:

```
[
    {"role": "user", "content": "What is OSPF?"},
    {"role": "assistant", "content": "OSPF is a link-state routing protocol..."}
]
```

This structure should look familiar if you have used modern chat APIs. Even though this lab calls the Ollama generate endpoint directly, the principle is the same: the application stores the conversation and decides what context to send.

The full memory pattern is shown in *Figure 5.2*. The user message and assistant response are appended to history, and the next prompt is built from that history:

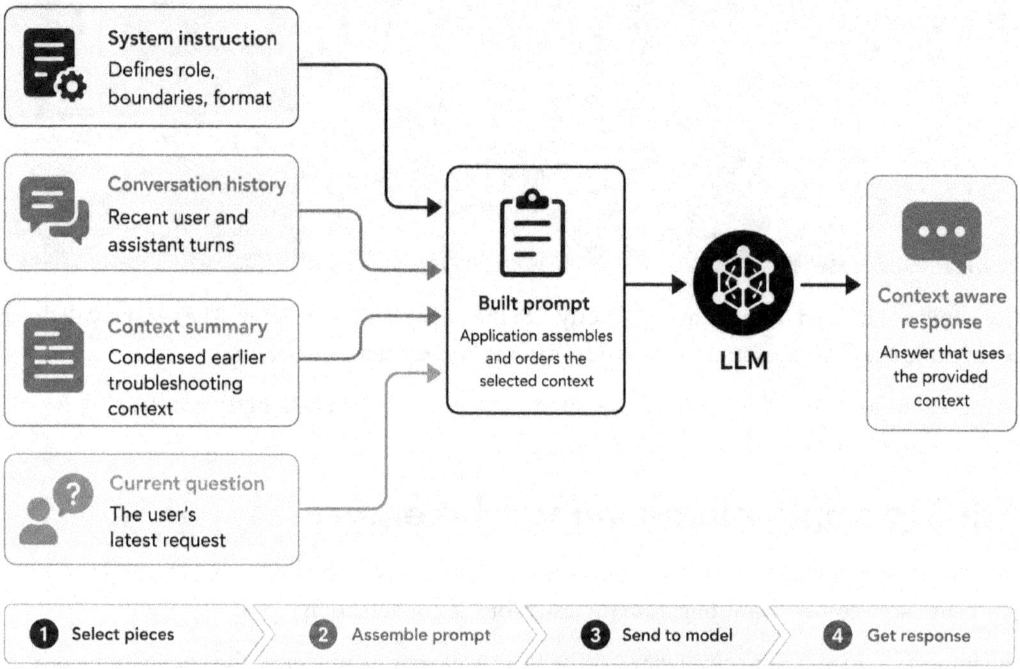

Figure 5.2: Building a prompt from conversation history

Once this pattern is in place, the chatbot can answer follow-up questions because the previous turn is inside the prompt. We are still not using a database, retrieval system, or vector search. For this chapter, a simple list is enough.

Building the NetworkChatbot class

The stateful chatbot wraps the logic inside a `NetworkChatbot` class. That gives the chatbot a place to store the model name, the conversation history, and the system prompt.

The setup begins in the `__init__()` method:

```
class NetworkChatbot:
    """Chatbot with conversation memory for network engineering."""

    def __init__(self, model: str = "llama3.2:3b"):
        self.model = model
        self.conversation_history = []
        self.system_prompt = """You are a network engineer assistant.
```

```
Available devices:
- spine1, spine2 (core switches)
- leaf1, leaf2 (access switches)

Provide accurate, concise answers about networking."""
```

There are three important pieces here. The model is still `llama3.2:3b`. The history starts as an empty list. The system prompt tells the assistant how to behave and gives it a small amount of network context.

This is where the chatbot starts to feel more like a network assistant. The model is not just answering generic questions. It is being guided to answer as a network engineering assistant with a small set of known devices.

Building the chat method

The `chat()` method is where most of the work happens. It appends the user message, builds the full prompt, calls Ollama, stores the response, and returns the response to the caller.

The core flow looks like this:

```
def chat(self, user_message: str)-> str:
    """Send message with full conversation history."""
    self.conversation_history.append({
        "role": "user",
        "content": user_message
    })

    full_prompt = self._build_prompt()

    payload = {
        "model": self.model,
        "prompt": full_prompt,
        "stream": False,
        "options": {
            "temperature": 0.7,
            "num_predict": 1024
        }
    }

    response = requests.post(
        "http://localhost:11434/api/generate",
        json=payload,
```

```
        timeout=60
    )
    response.raise_for_status()
    assistant_message = response.json().get("response", "")

    self.conversation_history.append({
        "role": "assistant",
        "content": assistant_message
    })

    return assistant_message
```

The model still receives text. The difference is that the text now includes the current user message plus previous conversation context. That is the memory pattern.

Building the full prompt

The helper method `_build_prompt()` converts the message history into one prompt that Ollama can process. It starts with the system prompt, then appends each user and assistant message in order.

The function looks like this:

```
def _build_prompt(self)-> str:
    """Build prompt with system message and conversation history."""
    prompt_parts = [self.system_prompt, "\n\n"]

    for msg in self.conversation_history:
        if msg["role"] == "user":
            prompt_parts.append(f"User: {msg['content']}\n")
        elif msg["role"] == "assistant":
            prompt_parts.append(f"Assistant: {msg['content']}\n")

    prompt_parts.append("Assistant: ")
    return "".join(prompt_parts)
```

This is a simple design, and that is the point. Before we add databases, summaries, retrieval, or tools, we should understand the basic pattern: history becomes prompt context.

Running the memory-enabled chatbot

Now run the second script from the repository root:

```
python3 labs/lab3-chatbot/chatbot_v2_with_memory.py
```

A successful run should look similar to this. The model wording will vary, but the second answer should show that the chatbot has access to the earlier question:

```
🤖 Stateful Chatbot Demo (Ollama)
======================================================================

👤 User: What is OSPF?
🤖 Bot: OSPF is a link-state routing protocol...

👤 User: What did I just ask you?
🤖 Bot: You asked what OSPF is.

✅ SUCCESS: The bot remembers!
   Conversation length: 4 messages

======================================================================
💬 Interactive Mode - Type 'quit' to exit, 'reset' to clear history
======================================================================
```

The conversation length is four messages because the application stored two user messages and two assistant messages. That count matters. It confirms that state is accumulating in the application, not inside the model.

From here, the script enters interactive mode. You can ask follow-up questions, reset the conversation, or exit the chatbot. This is still a simple command line chatbot, but it has the core behavior we need for later chapters.

Managing conversation history

Conversation history is useful, but it is also something we have to manage. Every message we keep can be sent back to the model. That means the history consumes part of the context window we discussed in *Chapter 2*.

For a short lab, sending the full history is fine. For a long troubleshooting session, the history can grow quickly. If the user pastes command output, logs, or long summaries into the chat, the prompt can become large before you notice.

The following table compares common memory strategies we will reuse as the book progresses:

Strategy	How it works	When to use it
Full history	Send every prior message in the session	Small labs and short conversations
Recent history	Keep only the latest messages	Interactive troubleshooting sessions
Summary memory	Summarize older messages and keep recent turns verbatim	Longer sessions with important context
External storage	Save context in files, databases, or retrieval systems	Production applications and multi-session assistants

Table 5.1: Common chatbot memory strategies

For now, the lab uses full history because it is the easiest way to see how memory works. Later, as we add tools and richer network data, we will be more selective about what the assistant carries forward.

Resetting the conversation

The stateful chatbot also includes a `reset()` method. This is small but important. A user should be able to clear the history when the topic changes or when previous context starts to pollute the conversation.

The reset method is intentionally simple:

```
def reset(self):
    """Clear conversation history."""
    self.conversation_history = []
```

In interactive mode, typing `reset` calls this method and clears the stored messages. That gives the user a clean slate without restarting the program.

This might sound like a convenience feature, but it is also a safety feature. Old context can mislead the model. Clearing state is one way to keep the assistant focused.

Using a network-focused system prompt

The **system prompt** gives the chatbot its operating behavior. In this lab, the system prompt tells the model to act as a network engineer assistant and gives it a small inventory of devices.

The prompt in the script is short on purpose:

```
You are a network engineer assistant.

Available devices:
- spine1, spine2 (core switches)
- leaf1, leaf2 (access switches)

Provide accurate, concise answers about networking.
```

A system prompt does not guarantee perfect behavior, but it gives the model a starting frame. It also becomes a useful place to set expectations such as keeping answers concise, avoiding unsupported claims, and asking for more context when needed.

Do not confuse a system prompt with a security boundary. It helps shape behavior, but your code still needs validation, tool permissions, and guardrails. We will reinforce that point when we move from chatbot memory into tool calling.

Preparing chatbot memory for agents

At this point, we have a chatbot that can remember a short conversation. That is useful, but it is still not an agent. It cannot check a device, inspect logs, or call a tool. It can only respond using the prompt context we provide.

That is exactly where we want to be before the next step. Memory gives the assistant continuity. Tool calling gives it controlled access to outside information. When we combine those two ideas, the assistant can maintain troubleshooting context while also asking for current network state.

For example, a future troubleshooting flow might look like this:

- The user reports that a BGP neighbor is down on `leaf1`
- The assistant remembers the device and neighbor from earlier turns
- The assistant calls a read-only tool to check interface status

- The assistant adds the result to the conversation context
- The assistant explains the likely cause using the gathered evidence

This is why memory matters. Without it, every tool call and follow-up question becomes disconnected. With it, the assistant can carry the thread of the investigation forward.

> **Tip**
>
> The repository also includes `chatbot_v3_live_ssh.py`, which extends the chatbot pattern toward live device access. This chapter keeps the main flow focused on local chatbot memory because live SSH introduces credentials, device reachability, command safety, timeouts, and environment-specific behavior. Treat the live SSH version as an advanced extension after you are comfortable with the memory pattern.

Checking production reality

A memory-enabled chatbot is closer to a real assistant, but production memory needs more care than a Python list. If the chatbot stores user messages, device names, logs, or incident details, that data becomes operational information. It may need retention rules, access control, and auditability.

There are also quality concerns. A long conversation can contain stale assumptions. The user may change topics. The assistant may carry forward an earlier mistake. That is why production systems often combine recent history, summaries, and retrieval rather than blindly sending everything back to the model.

The safest habit is to be explicit about memory. Know what you store. Know what you send. Know when to clear it. And before any tool call or risky action, validate the current context instead of assuming the conversation history is correct.

The same principle from earlier chapters still applies: useful, but controlled. Memory makes the assistant better, but it also gives us more responsibility.

Summary

In this chapter, we moved from a stateless chatbot to a memory-enabled network assistant. The stateless version showed the failure mode clearly: every call was independent, so follow-up questions failed. The stateful version fixed that by storing conversation history in the application and sending that history back with each new request.

We also looked at the `NetworkChatbot` class, the `chat()` method, the `_build_prompt()` method, the system prompt, reset behavior, and common memory strategies. The main lesson is simple: the model does not remember by itself. The application is doing that work.

This chapter gives us the next building block in the agent architecture. We now have local model calls, structured prompting, parsing patterns, and application-managed memory. In the next chapter, we will add controlled tools so the assistant can begin gathering current network state instead of only talking about it.

Get this book's PDF version and more

Scan the QR code (or go to `packtpub.com/unlock`). Search for this book by name, confirm the edition, and then follow the steps on the page.

UNLOCK NOW

Note: Keep your invoice handy. Purchases made directly from Packt don't require an invoice.

6

Designing Tools and Agentic Workflows

A chatbot with memory can remember what you asked before. That is useful, but it still cannot check a device, inspect a neighbor, or look up current network state on its own. At some point, a network assistant needs a safe way to ask for information from outside the model.

This is where *tool calling* enters the picture. The model does not get direct access to your routers. It does not open a shell and start typing commands. Instead, your application exposes a small set of approved functions. The model can request one of those functions, your code decides whether the request is allowed, and the result is passed back into the conversation.

That difference matters. An agent is not useful because it can do anything. It becomes useful when it can do a few narrow things safely, observe the results, and continue the investigation with evidence. That is the practical line between a chatbot that talks about networks and an agent that can help with network operations.

In this chapter, we will build that mental model using the local Ollama workflow and the mock network tools from the repository. We will focus on read-only actions, structured tool requests, safe Python execution, and loop limits. By the end, you will understand how the agentic pattern works before we use it for deeper troubleshooting in the next chapter.

In this chapter, we will cover the following topics:

- Review the technical requirements for the agentic workflow lab
- Understand why agents need tools instead of only memory
- Review the mock network tools used by the bot
- Describe tools to the model with clear operating boundaries
- Parse model-requested tool calls safely

- Execute approved Python functions through a tool map
- Return tool results to the model for another reasoning step
- Limit the agent loop to avoid uncontrolled behavior
- Run the local agentic network bot
- Apply production safety patterns to tool-based agents

These topics move us from a memory-enabled chatbot to a controlled tool using an agent. The goal is still practical: build the smallest safe pattern that lets the assistant observe network state without giving the model unrestricted access.

Technical requirements

This chapter uses the Lab 4 agentic workflow from the Packt repository. The main path stays local and uses mock network data, so you do not need live devices, credentials, or a lab fabric to follow along.

You need the following tools and files:

- Python 3.10 or later
- Ollama installed and running
- The `llama3.2:3b` model pulled locally
- The repository dependencies installed from `requirements.txt`
- The main script at `labs/lab4-agentic/agentic_network_bot_ollama.py`
- The mock network backend at `examples/mock_network_devices.py`
- The Lab 4 notes in `labs/lab4-agentic/README.md`

If you completed the setup from *Chapter 2*, you should already have most of this in place. From the repository root, you can run the main Lab 4 script with the following command:

```
python3 labs/lab4-agentic/agentic_network_bot_ollama.py
```

This chapter uses that file as the source of truth. The repository also contains live network variants, but we will treat those as optional advanced paths. The main teaching flow stays with mock read-only tools, so the behavior is repeatable for every reader.

Understanding why agents need tools

The chatbot we built in the previous chapter had memory. It could carry troubleshooting context across turns, which is a big step forward. But memory does not give the assistant current network state. If the user asks whether a BGP session is up right now, the model cannot know that from training data or conversation history alone.

The assistant needs a controlled way to ask the application for information. That is the role of a tool. In this book, a tool is a Python function that performs one narrow task, such as returning device status, checking interface state, retrieving a BGP summary, or testing reachability in the mock topology.

This is not the same as letting the model run arbitrary commands. The application decides which functions exist, which arguments they accept, and what they return. The model can request a tool, but your code owns execution. That separation is the safety boundary.

A simple example makes the point. If a user asks whether all BGP sessions are healthy, a generic chatbot can explain how BGP works. A tool-using agent can inspect the mock device data, discover that one peer is idle, and report that result with evidence. That is a different kind of workflow.

The loop we are building in this chapter is the foundation of **agentic workflows**. The agent observes the request, reasons about what information it needs, asks for a tool, receives the result, and decides whether it has enough evidence to answer or needs another tool call.

Figure 6.1 shows the basic loop we will use throughout this chapter:

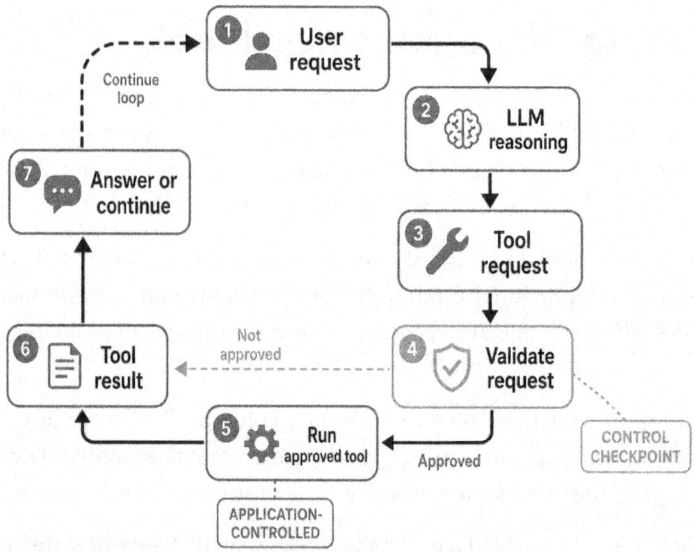

Figure 6.1: Tool calling loop in an agentic network workflow

The important point is that the loop is not magic. It is application code wrapped around model output. The model suggests the next step, but the application validates and executes the step.

Moving from chatbot responses to tool-assisted reasoning

The key change from *Chapter 5* is that the assistant no longer has to answer from the prompt alone. It can request a tool when it needs fresh or structured information. That does not make the model smarter by itself; it gives the model a better input.

In the Lab 4 script, the **AgenticNetworkBot** class stores the model name, conversation history, available tools, and the agent loop. The class still calls Ollama through a local **application programming interface** (**API**), but now the prompt includes a list of tools the model may request.

This design gives us a useful separation:

- The model decides what information would help answer the user request
- The application checks whether the requested tool exists
- The Python function executes the approved tool

- The tool result is added back into the conversation history
- The model reasons over the result and either asks for another tool or provides a final answer

That separation keeps the workflow understandable. When something goes wrong, you can inspect the model request, the tool arguments, the tool result, and the final answer as separate pieces.

Reviewing the mock network tools

Before we look at the agent loop, we need to understand the tools it can call. The file `examples/mock_network_devices.py` provides a small, simulated data center topology. It models two spine switches and two leaf switches, along with interface and BGP state.

The mock topology looks like this:

```
spine1 (192.168.0.11) ─┬─ leaf1 (192.168.0.21)
                       └─ leaf2 (192.168.0.22)
spine2 (192.168.0.12) ─┘
```

This is enough to demonstrate the pattern without requiring Containerlab, Arista `cEOS`, SSH credentials, or physical network devices. The mock data is realistic enough for learning, but safe enough for every reader to run.

The main tools available to the bot are summarized in *Table 6.1*:

Tool	What it returns	Why it is safe in the lab
`get_device_status()`	Device inventory and status	Read only mock data
`get_interface_status()`	Interface state and details	Read only mock data
`get_bgp_summary()`	BGP peers and states	Read only mock data
`ping_device()`	Reachability result	Mock test only
`execute_command()`	Allowed `show` command output	Show commands only
`get_topology_info()`	Topology metadata	Static data only

Table 6.1: Available mock network tools used by the agentic bot

The safety lesson is built into the lab. Even the generic command tool only allows show commands. That habit matters later when we move toward real device integrations.

Reviewing the main Lab 4 script

The main script for this chapter is `labs/lab4-agentic/agentic_network_bot_ollama.py`. It imports the mock tools, exposes them through a tool map, describes them to the model, and runs a loop that lets the model request tools.

The import section tells us which mock functions the agent can use:

```
from mock_network_devices import (
    get_device_status,
    get_interface_status,
    get_bgp_summary,
    ping_device,
    execute_command,
    get_topology_info
)
```

Those imports are the bridge between the agent and the simulated network. The model does not import or call these functions directly. The Python application does that through an approved mapping.

Mapping tool names to approved Python functions

Inside the agent class, the application creates a dictionary that maps tool names to Python functions. This is one of the most important safety controls in the chapter. The model can only request names that the application recognizes.

The tool map follows this pattern:

```
self.tools_map = {
    "get_device_status": get_device_status,
    "get_interface_status": get_interface_status,
    "get_bgp_summary": get_bgp_summary,
    "ping_device": ping_device,
    "execute_command": execute_command,
    "get_topology_info": get_topology_info
}
```

Figure 6.2 shows the relationship between the model request and the approved Python function map:

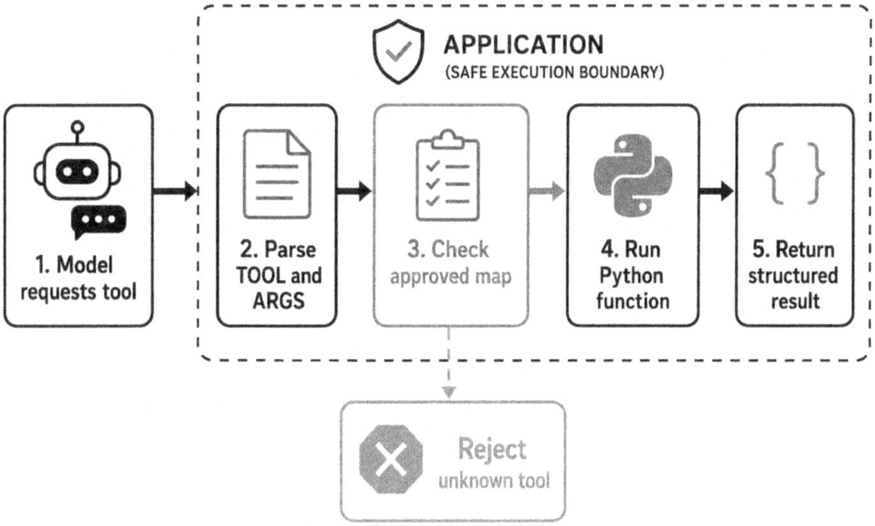

Figure 6.2: Mapping model-requested tools to approved Python functions

This mapping is why the agent is controlled. The model can produce text that asks for a tool, but the application decides whether that name points to a real function. If the name is not approved, nothing runs.

Describing tools to the model

The model needs to know what tools are available. In systems with native function calling, this might be done with formal tool schemas. In this local Ollama version, the script uses a structured prompt. That keeps the lab free and easy to run.

The script describes tools in plain language, including the function name, purpose, and example usage. A shortened example looks like this:

```
Available Tools:

1. get_device_status(device)
   - Get device info (hostname, version, uptime, role)
   - Example: get_device_status("spine1")

2. get_interface_status(device, interface)
   - Get interface state, IP, MAC
   - Example: get_interface_status("leaf1", "Ethernet1")
```

```
3. get_bgp_summary(device)
   - Get BGP neighbor status
   - Example: get_bgp_summary("spine1")
```

Good tool descriptions are not decoration. They affect whether the model picks the right tool, passes the right arguments, and stops when it has enough information. Vague tool descriptions create vague agent behavior.

The descriptions should answer three practical questions for the model:

- What does this tool do?
- When should this tool be used?
- What arguments does this tool expect?

That is enough for this lab. In a production system, you would usually make this stricter with structured tool definitions, type checks, argument validation, and permission checks.

Building the system prompt for tool use

The system prompt tells the model how to behave as a network assistant. It also tells the model how to request a tool. This is important because Ollama, in this lab flow, is not using native function calling. The application expects the model to output a specific text format.

The tool request format is intentionally simple:

```
TOOL: tool_name
ARGS: {"arg1": "value1", "arg2": "value2"}
```

The prompt then tells the model what to do after it receives tool results. It can either request another tool or provide a final answer. That is the agentic behavior. The model is not just answering once; it can take another step based on evidence.

A simplified version of the system prompt looks like this:

```
You are an expert network engineer troubleshooting a data center network.

When you need information, output a tool call in this EXACT format:
TOOL: tool_name
ARGS: {"arg1": "value1", "arg2": "value2"}

After getting tool results, analyze them and either:
1. Call another tool if you need more info
```

```
2. Provide your final answer

Be concise and practical. Focus on solving problems.
```

The word exact is doing real work here. If the model returns a tool request in the wrong shape, the parser may not recognize it. Later, we will talk about why native tool calling and Model Context Protocol can make this cleaner, but the plain text pattern is useful for learning the mechanics.

Parsing model requested tool calls

Once the model responds, the application has to decide whether the response contains a tool call or a final answer. The script does this with the `_parse_tool_call()` method.

The expected model output looks like this:

```
TOOL: get_device_status
ARGS: {"device": "spine1"}
```

The parser scans the response line by line, looks for a line that starts with `TOOL:`, looks for another line that starts with `ARGS:`, and then attempts to parse the arguments as JSON.

The simplified parsing logic looks like this:

```
def _parse_tool_call(self, response: str):
    lines = response.split("\n")
    tool_name = None
    tool_args = {}

    for line in lines:
        line = line.strip()
        if line.startswith("TOOL:"):
            tool_name = line.replace("TOOL:", "").strip()
        elif line.startswith("ARGS:"):
            args_str = line.replace("ARGS:", "").strip()
            tool_args = json.loads(args_str)

    if tool_name and tool_name in self.tools_map:
        return {"name": tool_name, "args": tool_args}

    return None
```

This parser is intentionally small. It is not the final production pattern. It teaches the core idea: model output is text until the application recognizes it, validates it, and turns it into a controlled action.

Executing tools safely

After the application parses a valid tool request, it still should not blindly execute anything. The script uses `tools_map` to look up the Python function by name, then passes the parsed arguments to that function.

The execution pattern is short:

```
def _execute_tool(self, tool_name: str, args: dict)-> dict:
    tool_func = self.tools_map[tool_name]

    try:
        result = tool_func(**args)
        return result if isinstance(result, dict) else {"result": str(result)}
    except TypeError as e:
        return {"error": f"Invalid arguments for {tool_name}: {str(e)}"}
```

The error handling here matters. If the model calls a real tool with the wrong arguments, the script should return a structured error instead of crashing. In production, you would add stricter validation before execution, but even this lab version teaches an important habit: tool calls need guardrails.

The `execute_command()` function in the mock backend also demonstrates a simple command boundary. It only allows commands that begin with show. That is not a complete security model, but it reinforces the right instinct for network operations: read only first.

Returning tool results to the model

A tool result is only useful if the model can inspect it. After a tool runs, the script serializes the result as JSON, prints it for the reader, and adds it back into the conversation history.

The pattern looks like this inside the loop:

```
result = self._execute_tool(tool_name, tool_args)
result_str = json.dumps(result, indent=2)

self.conversation_history.append({
    "role": "assistant",
```

```
        "content": f"TOOL: {tool_name}\nARGS: {json.dumps(tool_args)}"
    })

    self.conversation_history.append({
        "role": "user",
        "content": f"Tool result:\n{result_str}"
    })
```

This is where *Chapter 5* and *Chapter 6* connect. The application managed memory from *Chapter 5* is now carrying tool results forward. The next model call sees the user request, the tool request, and the tool result. That gives the model evidence to reason over.

The model can then decide whether it has enough information to answer or whether it needs another tool. That is the difference between a one-step script and an agentic loop.

Limiting the agent loop

Any loop that lets a model request more work needs a limit. Without a limit, a bad prompt or confused model could keep asking for tools until the process times out or consumes unnecessary resources.

The `chat()` method includes a `max_iterations` setting for this reason:

```
def chat(self, user_message: str, max_iterations: int = 5)-> str:
```

Each time the model requests a tool, the loop counter increases. If the model stops requesting tools, the response is treated as the final answer. If the loop reaches the maximum number of iterations, the application stops the loop and makes one final call.

A limit like this is not just a programming convenience. It is a safety boundary. Production agents need stronger controls, but the idea starts here: agents should not be allowed to run forever because the model keeps asking for another step.

Handling tool-calling failure modes

Tool calling introduces new failure modes. Some are boring, such as a typo in a device name. Some are more serious, such as a model requesting a command that should not run. The safest approach is to treat every model-requested action as untrusted until the application checks it.

Table 6.2 summarizes common failure modes and the safeguards that should be added around each one:

Failure mode	Example	Safeguard
Unknown tool name	The model requests `get_route_status()`, but no such tool exists	Reject the request and return a clear tool not found error
Bad arguments	The model passes `device=core1` when only `spine1`, `spine2`, `leaf1`, and `leaf2` exist	Validate device names before execution
Malformed `JSON` arguments	`ARGS` contains invalid JSON syntax	Return a parse error and ask the model to retry in the required format
Unsupported command	The model asks `execute_command()` to run `configure terminal`	Allow only read only `show` commands
Runaway loop	The model keeps asking for more tools without answering	Use `max_iterations` and stop safely
Messy tool output	The tool returns an error or incomplete data	Pass the error back clearly and avoid unsupported conclusions

Table 6.2: Tool calling failure modes and safeguards

This table is not meant to scare you away from agents. It is meant to keep the pattern honest. A good agent is still software, and software needs boring checks around the interesting parts.

Running the agentic network bot

Now that we understand the pieces, we can run the Lab 4 bot. Make sure Ollama is running and the `llama3.2:3b` model is available locally. Then run the script from the repository root:

```
python3 labs/lab4-agentic/agentic_network_bot_ollama.py
```

The script starts with a few test scenarios and then enters interactive mode. The exact model response can vary, but the structure should look similar to this:

```
🤖 Agentic Network Bot - Ollama Edition
======================================================================
No API keys required! Using Ollama (llama3.2:3b)
======================================================================

🎯 Running test scenarios...

======================================================================
👤 User: What's the status of spine1?
======================================================================

🔧 Agent is calling: get_device_status({"device": "spine1"})
📊 Result:
{
  "device": "spine1",
  "ip": "192.168.0.11",
  "status": "up",
  "model": "cEOS",
  "version": "4.28.0F",
  "uptime": "5d",
  "role": "spine"
}

🤖 Agent: spine1 is up and operating as a spine switch. It is running cEOS 4.28.0F
and has been up for 5 days.
```

The most important part of this output is the visible tool call. The agent did not simply guess that `spine1` was up. It requested `get_device_status()`, the application executed the approved Python function, and the model used that result to answer.

Trying a multi-step question

A single device status check is useful, but the agentic pattern becomes more interesting when the request requires more than one piece of information. In interactive mode, try asking this:

```
Are all BGP sessions up?
```

The agent may call `get_bgp_summary()` for one or more devices, inspect the peer states, and then summarize whether any sessions are not established. Because `leaf2` contains one idle BGP neighbor in the mock data, this is a useful test for evidence-based reporting.

A representative response may identify the idle neighbor and suggest checking the relevant link, interface state, or logs. The wording can vary, but the conclusion should be grounded in tool output rather than a generic explanation of BGP.

Testing an investigation query

The third built-in scenario asks the bot to check whether `leaf2` has issues. That query is useful because `leaf2` has a down server-facing interface and one BGP neighbor in the Idle state in the mock data.

A good agent should not jump straight to a final answer. It should inspect device status, BGP state, interface state, or topology information before summarizing what looks wrong. That is the agentic behavior we want readers to notice.

Keeping live network access optional

The repository includes files for exploring live network access later, such as `labs/lab4-agentic/lab4b_agentic_network_bot_netmiko.py` and `labs/lab4-agentic/live_network_devices.py`. This chapter does not make those files part of the main lab flow.

That is intentional. Live device access introduces credentials, device reachability, command safety, timeouts, vendor differences, and reader environment differences. Those are real concerns, but they are not the lesson of this chapter.

The main lesson here is tool design and the agentic loop. Once that is clear, live access can be treated as an advanced path with proper setup instructions, safe credential handling, and stronger validation.

Applying production boundaries to tools using agents

The Lab 4 bot is a learning implementation. It is not something we should point at production and trust blindly. But the design habits are the right ones: small tools, clear tool descriptions, controlled execution, visible output, and loop limits.

Table 6.3 shows how to think about the difference between the lab behavior and what a production-aware version would need:

Area	Lab behavior	Production direction
Tool access	Python functions call mock data	Use allowlisted read only APIs or SSH commands
Arguments	Basic parsing and `TypeError` handling	Validate device names, command names, values, and user permissions
Commands	Mock `execute_command()` allows `show` commands only	Use command allowlists and role-based access control
Secrets	No credentials required	Use environment variables or a secrets manager
Logging	Tool calls are printed to the terminal	Write structured logs with user, tool, args, result status, and duration
Loop limits	`max_iterations` prevents endless loops	Add per user limits, rate limits, and timeout policies
Write actions	No configuration changes	Require human approval, audit logs, and rollback planning

Table 6.3: Moving from lab tool calling to production-aware boundaries

The production version is not just the same script with real credentials added. That is the part people usually underestimate. Once tools touch real systems, you need stronger boundaries around every step.

Logging what the agent does

A tool-using agent should leave a trail. If the agent calls `get_bgp_summary()` and then `get_interface_status()`, an engineer should be able to see that sequence later. Without that trail, debugging the agent becomes harder than debugging the network.

Even in this lab, the script prints the tool name, arguments, and result. That is a good starting habit. A production system should record that information as structured logs, along with the user, timestamp, duration, success or failure, and any approval decision.

Logging also helps with trust. Engineers are more likely to use an assistant that shows what it checked. If the final answer includes evidence from the tool results, it becomes easier to validate and easier to challenge when something looks wrong.

Avoiding common agent design mistakes

The first mistake is giving the agent too many tools too early. More tools do not automatically make the agent better. They make the decision space larger. Start with a few tools that map to real operational questions, then add more when you understand the failure modes.

The second mistake is hiding tool execution. If the reader or operator cannot see which tool was called and what came back, the agent becomes a black box. That is not what we want in network operations.

The third mistake is using tools to bypass good automation. If you already have a script that reliably checks an interface, keep it. Expose that script as a tool. Let the agent decide when to ask for it, but keep deterministic work deterministic.

The fourth mistake is skipping validation because the demo looked good once. Demos are friendly. Production is not. Tool names, arguments, command output, device names, and final conclusions all need checks.

Preparing for the main troubleshooting agent

At this point, we have the building blocks for an agentic workflow. We can describe tools, parse model-requested tool calls, execute approved Python functions, return results to the model, and stop the loop when needed.

The next step is to use those pieces in a more complete troubleshooting story. Instead of only showing tool mechanics, we will start with a realistic operational problem and let the agent work through the evidence. That is where the pattern becomes useful for network operations.

Chapter 7 will build on this foundation. The agent will still be controlled, still read-only, and still backed by mock data first. The difference is that we will focus more on the end-to-end investigation rather than the individual mechanics.

Summary

In this chapter, we moved from a memory-enabled chatbot to a tool-using agent. We saw why memory is not enough when the assistant needs current network state, and we introduced tools as controlled Python functions that expose specific information to the model.

We reviewed the mock network topology, the available tool functions, the tool map, the structured `TOOL` and `ARGS` format, and the application loop that executes tools and returns results to the model. We also covered why loop limits, validation, and clear tool boundaries matter.

The key takeaway is simple: the model is not the executor. The application is. The model can request information, but your code decides what tools exist, whether the request is valid, and how results flow back into the conversation.

In the next chapter, we will use this tool-calling foundation to build a fuller network troubleshooting agent. Instead of asking whether the agent can call a tool, we will ask whether it can follow a practical investigation path and return evidence an engineer can trust.

Join us on Discord

For discussions around the book and to connect with your peers, join us on Discord at `packt.link/discordcloud` or scan the QR code below:

7

Building the Main Network Troubleshooting Agent

In the last chapter, we built the mechanics of a tool-using agent. The model could request a tool, the application could check the request, the approved Python function could run, and the result could be returned to the model. That pattern is useful, but it is still only the machinery.

This chapter turns that machinery into a troubleshooting workflow. Instead of asking whether the agent can call a tool, we will ask whether it can follow evidence through a network problem. The scenario is practical: a BGP issue that may explain a missing route or unreachable host symptom.

The important point is not that the agent magically solves the network. It does not. The useful part is that it can gather current state from mock tools, compare the evidence, and produce a better starting point for the engineer. The engineer still owns the decision. The application still owns execution. The model helps reason over the evidence.

We will keep this chapter local, mocked, and read-only. That makes the investigation repeatable for every reader and keeps the focus where it belongs: building an evidence-driven troubleshooting pattern before we talk about reusable tool packaging in the next chapter.

In this chapter, we will cover the following topics:

- Reviewing the technical requirements for the troubleshooting agent
- Understanding how *Chapter 6* becomes a troubleshooting workflow
- Reviewing the mock topology and evidence sources
- Running the main agent script
- Investigating device status as a warm-up
- Investigating BGP neighbor health

- Using reachability checks for a missing route to host symptom
- Correcting model conclusions with tool evidence
- Designing a stronger troubleshooting response
- Keeping the workflow mocked, read-only, and safe
- Preparing the agent for reusable tooling in the next chapter

By the end of this chapter, you will have a clearer view of what a practical network troubleshooting agent should do. It should gather facts, expose its evidence, avoid unsupported conclusions, and give the engineer a useful next step.

Technical requirements

This chapter uses the same local setup from the earlier labs. You should have Ollama running locally, the repository dependencies installed, and the `deepseek-r1:8b` model available for the Lab 4 troubleshooting agent.

The main troubleshooting workflow in this chapter uses the same Lab 4 agentic bot that introduced tool calling in the previous chapter. We are reusing it here because the goal is to focus on the investigation path, not introduce another tool framework yet.

You need the following tools and files:

- Python 3.10 or later
- Ollama installed and running
- The `deepseek-r1:8b` model available locally for the troubleshooting agent
- The repository dependencies installed from `requirements.txt`
- The main script at `labs/lab4-agentic/agentic_network_bot_ollama.py`
- The mock network backend at `examples/mock_network_devices.py`
- The Lab 4 notes in `labs/lab4-agentic/README.md`

Before running the troubleshooting agent, pull the model used by the latest Lab 4 script:

```
ollama pull deepseek-r1:8b
```

After the model is available, run the main script from the repository root:

```
python3 labs/lab4-agentic/agentic_network_bot_ollama.py
```

The chapter stays with mock data. There is no live device access, no credentials, and no configuration change path. That keeps the examples safe and repeatable.

Moving from tool mechanics to troubleshooting

Chapter 6 explained the tool calling loop. A user sends a request, the model reasons about what information it needs, the model requests a tool, the application validates that request, and an approved Python function runs. That is the mechanical side of an agent.

Troubleshooting needs a little more discipline. The agent has to decide what evidence matters, call tools in a sensible order, compare results, and avoid claiming more than the data supports. In network operations, that last part matters as much as the tool call itself.

A useful troubleshooting agent should behave more like a careful junior engineer than a magic box. It should ask for the right facts, inspect the output, call out uncertainty, and explain why it reached a conclusion.

Figure 7.1 shows the troubleshooting loop we will use in this chapter:

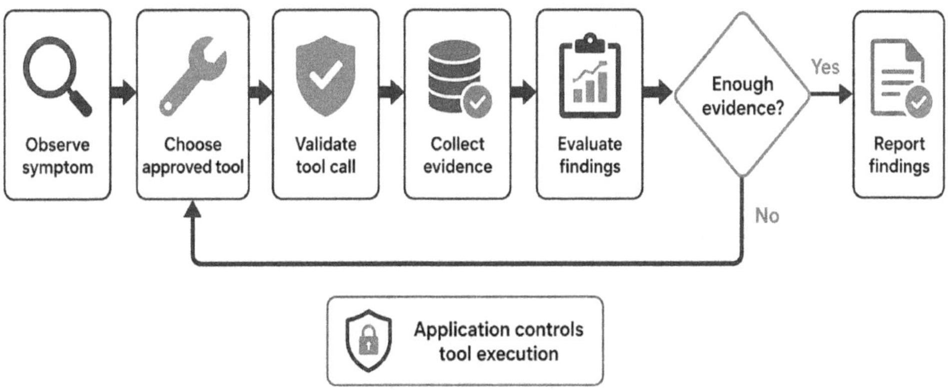

Figure 7.1: Evidence-driven troubleshooting loop for a network agent

The loop looks simple because it should be simple. The agent receives a symptom, gathers facts through approved tools, checks whether the facts support a conclusion, and either asks for more evidence or reports what it found. The model is not the executor. The application controls the tools.

Reviewing the troubleshooting scenarios

The main scenario for this chapter combines two common network symptoms: a BGP problem and a missing route to host or unreachable destination. In a real environment, those symptoms may or may not be related. That is why the agent should not jump to the first obvious answer.

A user may report that an application host is unreachable. A routing table may be missing a prefix. A monitoring alert may say that a BGP neighbor is down. The job of the troubleshooting agent is to gather enough evidence to say what is known, what looks suspicious, and what should be checked next.

The investigation path we will build toward uses the following evidence:

- Device status from `get_device_status()`
- Interface state from `get_interface_status()`
- BGP peer state from `get_bgp_summary()`
- Reachability results from `ping_device()`
- Topology context from `get_topology_info()`

Table 7.1 maps common troubleshooting questions to the supporting mock tools and the evidence each tool should provide:

Investigation question	**Supporting tool**	**What the agent should check**
Is the device reachable in the mock inventory?	`get_device_status()`	Device status, role, model, and management IP
Is the relevant interface up?	`get_interface_status()`	`status`, `description`, and `speed`
Are BGP peers established?	`get_bgp_summary()`	`total_peers`, `established_peers`, neighbor `state`, and `prefixes`
Is the target reachable?	`ping_device()`	`status`, `packet_loss`, and `error`
Does the topology explain the path?	`get_topology_info()`	Device roles, links, and known relationships

Table 7.1: Troubleshooting questions and supporting tools

The table is not a rigid runbook. It is a starting point. The agent can choose tools based on the question, but its final answer should always be grounded in the tool results.

Reviewing the mock topology

The repository uses a small mock data center topology. The exact topology is intentionally small, because the goal is to learn the investigation pattern without forcing every reader to build a live lab fabric.

The topology contains two spine switches and two leaf switches. The useful degraded case is `leaf2`, because its device status is up, its BGP summary includes one neighbor in the `Idle` state, and its interface list shows `Ethernet3` down. That gives us a realistic problem to investigate.

A simplified view of the topology looks like this:

```
spine1 (192.168.0.11) ─┬─ leaf1 (192.168.0.21)
                        └─ leaf2 (192.168.0.22)
spine2 (192.168.0.12) ─┘
```

Because the topology is mocked, you can safely rerun the same tests. If the model wording changes, the tool output should still give you the same evidence to reason over.

Running the troubleshooting agent

Start by running the main agent script from the repository root:

```
python3 labs/lab4-agentic/agentic_network_bot_ollama.py
```

The script starts in Ollama mode, runs built-in test scenarios, and then enters interactive mode. A representative startup looks like this:

```
🤖 Agentic Network Bot - Ollama Edition
======================================================================
No API keys required! Using Ollama (deepseek-r1:8b)
======================================================================

🎯 Running test scenarios...
```

The model output may vary from run to run because a local model is generating text. The important thing is the tool evidence. If the final wording changes, check whether the agent called the expected tools and whether the final answer matches the returned data.

Scenario 1: Checking device status

The first scenario is a warm-up. The user asks for the status of `spine1`. This is not a deep investigation, but it proves that the agent can request a tool, receive structured data, and use that result in a response.

The user request is simple:

```
What's the status of spine1?
```

A representative tool call looks like this:

```
🔧 Agent is calling: get_device_status({"device": "spine1"})
📊 Result:
{
  "device": "spine1",
  "ip": "192.168.0.11",
  "status": "up",
  "model": "cEOS",
  "version": "4.28.0F",
  "serial": "SPX2134567890",
  "uptime": "5d",
  "role": "spine"
}
```

The final answer should say that `spine1` is up and should mention supporting details such as role, model, version, or uptime. This is a good first test because the answer has a clear source: `get_device_status()` returned the facts.

Scenario 2: Checking BGP health

The next scenario is more interesting. The user asks whether all BGP sessions are up. A weak chatbot might answer by explaining how BGP works. The troubleshooting agent should inspect BGP state instead.

Try the following question in interactive mode:

```
Are all BGP sessions up?
```

A useful agent should call `get_bgp_summary()` for the relevant devices and inspect both the peer counts and each neighbor state. *Table 7.2* summarizes the fields the agent should check before drawing a conclusion:

Field	Meaning	How to interpret it
`total_peers`	Number of neighbors configured or known in the mock data	Compare it with `established_peers`
`established_peers`	Number of neighbors currently established	If this is lower than `total_peers`, there is at least one BGP issue
`state`	State for each individual BGP neighbor	Anything other than `Established` should be reported
`prefixes`	Number of prefixes received from the neighbor	A value of `0` may explain missing route symptoms
`uptime`	How long the session has been in its current state	Useful for identifying recent flaps or long-standing issues

Table 7.2: BGP fields the troubleshooting agent should inspect

The main rule is simple: the final answer must not contradict these fields. If a neighbor is `Idle`, the answer should say so. If `established_peers` is lower than `total_peers`, the answer should not say all sessions are healthy.

Scenario 3: Investigating leaf2

The built-in `leaf2` scenario is the most useful one in this chapter because it contains a degraded BGP state and a down interface. The device itself is up, one BGP neighbor is `Idle`, and the interface list shows that `Ethernet3` is down.

Try this question:

```
Check if leaf2 has any issues
```

The agent should gather evidence before answering. A representative sequence includes these tool calls:

```
🔧 Agent is calling: get_device_status({"device": "leaf2"})
🔧 Agent is calling: get_bgp_summary({"device": "leaf2"})
🔧 Agent is calling: get_interface_status({"device": "leaf2"})
```

The BGP result is the first important part of the investigation:

```
📊 Result:
{
  "device": "leaf2",
  "local_as": 65012,
  "router_id": "10.0.1.22",
  "total_peers": 2,
  "established_peers": 1,
  "neighbors": [
    {
      "ip": "10.1.1.2",
      "remote_as": 65001,
      "state": "Established",
      "uptime": "2d3h",
      "prefixes": 50
    },
    {
      "ip": "10.1.2.2",
      "remote_as": 65001,
      "state": "Idle",
      "uptime": "0h",
      "prefixes": 0
    }
  ]
}
```

The interface result adds the local interface evidence:

```
📊 Result:
{
  "device": "leaf2",
  "interfaces": [
    {
      "name": "Ethernet1",
      "description": "to_spine1",
      "status": "up",
      "speed": "10G"
    },
    {
      "name": "Ethernet2",
      "description": "to_spine2",
      "status": "up",
      "speed": "10G"
    },
    {
      "name": "Ethernet3",
      "description": "server_rack_2",
      "status": "down",
      "speed": "1G"
    },
    {
      "name": "Management1",
      "description": "oob_management",
      "status": "up",
      "speed": "1G"
    }
  ]
}
```

A correct final summary should separate healthy evidence from degraded evidence. `leaf2` is up, but the BGP summary shows only one established peer out of two, and the interface list shows `Ethernet3` down. The neighbor `10.1.2.2` is `Idle` and has 0 prefixes.

A good answer would look like this:

```
leaf2 is up, but there are two issues to investigate.
BGP has 1/2 peers Established.
Neighbor 10.1.2.2 is in Idle state and is receiving 0 prefixes.
Ethernet3 (server_rack_2) is down.
This may explain missing routes that depend on that peer, while Ethernet3 may
affect the server-facing segment.
Next checks: verify the peer path, interface toward the peer, recent logs, BGP
configuration, and the local server-facing interface state.
```

That answer is useful because it does not overstate the problem. It reports the facts, names the suspicious neighbor, includes the down local interface, and suggests practical next checks.

Scenario 4: Investigating a missing route to host symptom

A missing route to host symptom is often reported as a reachability failure. The exact root cause might be a routing problem, a failed neighbor, an interface problem, a firewall rule, or a missing advertisement. The agent should not assume BGP is the cause until the evidence supports that direction.

In the mock workflow, reachability is checked through `ping_device()`. The mock backend function accepts a `target` and an optional `count`. For example, a test can use a known device name or an unknown `target` to simulate reachability failure.

The missing route investigation can start with a user request like this:

```
Host 10.99.99.99 is unreachable. Check whether this could be related to BGP on
leaf2.
```

The agent should gather more than one piece of evidence. A reasonable investigation path is shown in *Figure 7.2*:

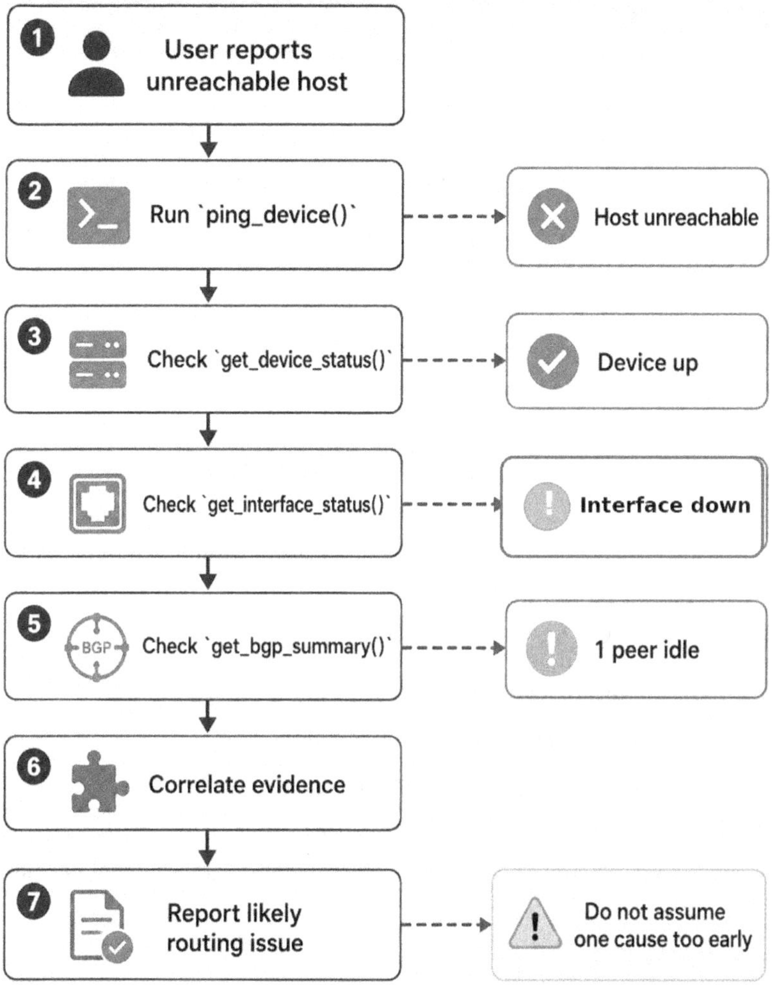

Figure 7.2: BGP and missing route to host investigation path

The reachability check may return an `unreachable` result for an unknown target:

```
🔧 Agent is calling: ping_device({"target": "10.99.99.99", "count": 4})
📊 Result:
{
  "target": "10.99.99.99",
  "packets_sent": 4,
  "packets_received": 0,
  "packet_loss": 100,
  "status": "unreachable",
```

```
    "error": "Destination host unreachable"
  }
```

That result proves reachability failed in the mock tool. It does not prove why. To connect the symptom to BGP, the agent still needs BGP evidence from `leaf2`. If `get_bgp_summary()` shows an `Idle` neighbor with 0 prefixes, the agent can say that the failed BGP session may be related to the missing route symptom. The interface result also shows `Ethernet3` down, so the server-facing segment should be checked separately.

The careful wording matters. A strong answer should say may be related or likely related based on the available evidence, not definitely caused by BGP unless the tool data proves the exact route is missing because of that neighbor.

Building an evidence-based final answer

The final answer is where many agent demos become misleading. The model may produce fluent text even when it misses a detail. That is dangerous in troubleshooting because a confident but wrong summary can waste time.

A stronger final answer should include four parts:

- Confirmed facts from tool output
- Evidence that looks unhealthy or inconsistent
- Likely cause or possible cause, clearly labeled
- Next checks the engineer should run or approve

Table 7.3 shows how each response element helps the agent produce a reliable troubleshooting answer:

Response element	Example	Why it matters
Confirmed facts	`leaf2` is up; `Ethernet3` is down	Separates known good state from the suspected issue
Unhealthy evidence	Neighbor `10.1.2.2` is `Idle` with 0 prefixes; `Ethernet3` is down	Points to the specific failure signal

Response element	Example	Why it matters
Likely cause	Missing routes may be related to the idle BGP neighbor; the server-facing segment may also be affected	Connects the symptom to evidence without overclaiming
Next checks	Check peer reachability, logs, BGP configuration, and `Ethernet3` state	Gives the engineer practical follow-up

Table 7.3: Recommended structure for an agent troubleshooting answer

This format is easy to read during an incident. It also makes the answer easier to review because the conclusion is tied to the tool output.

Catching wrong or incomplete model conclusions

One of the most important lessons in this chapter is that model conclusions need to be checked against tool evidence. The tool result may say one thing, while the generated summary says another. When that happens, the evidence should win.

For example, this is a risky conclusion:

```
leaf2 appears to be functioning normally. It has two established peers and no
major connectivity issues.
```

That conclusion is not safe if the tool output says `established_peers` is `1` and one neighbor is `Idle`. The response should be corrected to match the evidence:

```
leaf2 is up, but it has issues to investigate.
Only 1 of 2 BGP peers is established.
Neighbor 10.1.2.2 is Idle and receiving 0 prefixes.
Ethernet3 (server_rack_2) is down.
This may explain missing routes learned through that neighbor, while Ethernet3 may
affect the server-facing segment.
```

This is the reason we keep tool results visible. The engineer should be able to compare the final answer with the evidence and spot any mismatches quickly.

Improving the troubleshooting prompts

A better troubleshooting prompt can reduce these mistakes. It cannot remove the need for validation, but it can make the model more likely to produce useful operational answers.

The prompt should include rules such as these:

- Always compare `established_peers` with `total_peers`
- Always list any BGP neighbor whose state is not `Established`
- Mention `prefixes: 0` when it appears on a neighbor that may affect routing
- Do not say there are no issues if any tool result contains an error, an idle peer, a down interface, or an unreachable target
- Separate confirmed facts from likely causes
- Give next checks rather than claiming certainty when the tool data is incomplete

A tightened instruction block might look like this:

```
When summarizing troubleshooting results:
- Report any BGP neighbor not in Established state.
- Compare established_peers with total_peers.
- Treat prefixes: 0 as possible routing impact.
- Do not claim no issues if any tool returned an error or degraded state.
- Separate confirmed facts, likely causes, and next checks.
```

This looks like prompt engineering, but it is really operational discipline. We are telling the model what a network engineer would check before writing the summary.

Using the agent interactively

After the built-in tests complete, the script enters interactive mode. This is where you can try small variations of the troubleshooting scenario.

Useful test questions include:

- Check if `leaf2` has any BGP issues.
- Is neighbor `10.1.2.2` healthy?
- Host `10.99.99.99` is unreachable. What should I check?
- Could a failed BGP session explain missing routes on `leaf2`?
- Show the evidence before giving the conclusion.

When you test interactively, do not judge only the final paragraph. Watch the tool calls. A good troubleshooting agent should ask for evidence before answering, especially when the request is about the current state.

Table 7.4 lists practical reader tests and the behavior that shows whether the agent is using evidence correctly:

Reader test	Expected agent behavior	Warning sign
Check if `leaf2` has any BGP issues	Calls `get_bgp_summary()` and `get_interface_status()`, then reports the idle neighbor and `Ethernet3` down	Says `leaf2` is healthy without checking BGP
Host `10.99.99.99` is unreachable	Calls `ping_device()` and explains reachability failure	Assumes the cause without checking
Are all BGP sessions up?	Compares `total_peers` and `established_peers`	Only explains BGP in general terms
Show the evidence	Includes tool results or field names in the answer	Returns a vague recommendation

Table 7.4: Interactive tests for the troubleshooting agent

These tests help you evaluate the agent behavior, not just the model wording. If the model gives a nice answer without evidence, that is still a weak troubleshooting workflow.

Keeping the workflow mocked and read-only

This chapter intentionally keeps the workflow mocked and read-only. That decision is not a limitation of the idea. It is the right learning sequence.

Live network access introduces credentials, device reachability, vendor differences, timeouts, command safety, and environment-specific behavior. Those are real concerns, but they are not the focus of this chapter. The focus here is whether the agent can follow a troubleshooting path and explain evidence correctly.

The mock workflow still teaches the important habits:

- Expose only approved tools
- Prefer read-only data collection
- Show tool calls and results
- Check conclusions against structured output
- Stop the loop when enough evidence exists
- Avoid unsupported claims

Once those habits are solid, moving toward live tools becomes a production-readiness topic, not a *Chapter 7* requirement.

Understanding what the agent can and cannot do

A practical troubleshooting agent should make the engineer faster, not pretend to replace the engineer. The boundary is important because the agent can only reason over the context and tools we give it.

Table 7.5 summarizes what the mocked troubleshooting agent can support and what remains out of scope in this chapter:

Supported in this chapter	Out of scope in this chapter
Call approved mock tools	Connect to real devices
Inspect device, interface, BGP, topology, and reachability data	Guarantee live network state
Summarize likely causes from evidence	Prove causes that are not in the tool output
Suggest next checks	Make configuration changes
Expose tool evidence for review	Replace engineer judgment

Table 7.5: Capabilities and boundaries of the troubleshooting agent

This boundary keeps the agent useful. The reader should finish the chapter understanding what the pattern can do today and what must be added before it touches production.

Walking through the leaf2 investigation step by step

The `leaf2` case deserves a slower walkthrough because it demonstrates a common troubleshooting trap. A device can be up and still have a routing problem. An interface can be down and still not be the only issue. If the agent stops at the first signal, it can produce a comforting but incomplete answer.

The first layer of evidence is device state. In the mock data, `leaf2` is present and reported as up. That is useful, but it only tells us that the device itself is available in the simulated inventory. The first tool call and result look like this:

```
🔧 Agent is calling: get_device_status({"device": "leaf2"})
📊 Result:
{
  "device": "leaf2",
  "ip": "192.168.0.22",
  "status": "up",
  "model": "cEOS",
  "version": "4.27.3F",
  "serial": "LFX2134567891",
  "uptime": "2d",
  "role": "leaf"
}
```

A weak answer might stop here and say `leaf2` is healthy. That would be premature. A device can be reachable while one routing session is broken or while one prefix is missing.

The second layer is BGP state. This is where the degraded routing evidence appears:

```
🔧 Agent is calling: get_bgp_summary({"device": "leaf2"})
📊 Result:
{
  "device": "leaf2",
  "local_as": 65012,
  "router_id": "10.0.1.22",
  "total_peers": 2,
  "established_peers": 1,
  "neighbors": [
    {
      "ip": "10.1.1.2",
      "remote_as": 65001,
```

```
        "state": "Established",
        "uptime": "2d3h",
        "prefixes": 50
      },
      {
        "ip": "10.1.2.2",
        "remote_as": 65001,
        "state": "Idle",
        "uptime": "0h",
        "prefixes": 0
      }
    ]
  }
```

This BGP result shows that the device is up but routing is not fully healthy.

The third layer is interface state. The agent asks for the full interface list so it does not miss local interface problems:

```
🔧 Agent is calling: get_interface_status({"device": "leaf2"})
📊 Result:
{
  "device": "leaf2",
  "interfaces": [
    {
      "name": "Ethernet1",
      "description": "to_spine1",
      "status": "up",
      "speed": "10G"
    },
    {
      "name": "Ethernet2",
      "description": "to_spine2",
      "status": "up",
      "speed": "10G"
    },
    {
      "name": "Ethernet3",
      "description": "server_rack_2",
      "status": "down",
      "speed": "1G"
```

```
    },
    {
      "name": "Management1",
      "description": "oob_management",
      "status": "up",
      "speed": "1G"
    }
  ]
}
```

Now the conclusion must include both degraded signals. The correct finding is not simply that `leaf2` is up. The correct finding is that `leaf2` is up, one BGP neighbor is `Idle` with `0` prefixes, and `Ethernet3` is down.

A useful agent should preserve that contrast. Healthy device state and unhealthy routing or interface state can exist at the same time. That is why an evidence-based answer should include both.

Creating an evidence record

The current lab stores tool calls and results in conversation history. That is enough for the model to reason over the investigation. A more mature implementation could also keep a structured evidence record outside the model prompt.

An evidence record gives the application something deterministic to inspect. It can record what was checked, which tool produced the result, and which fields looked unhealthy. This makes the final answer easier to audit and easier to validate.

For the `leaf2` case, an evidence record might look like this:

```
{
  "device": "leaf2",
  "evidence": {
    "device_status": {
      "tool": "get_device_status",
      "status": "up"
    },
    "interface_status": {
      "tool": "get_interface_status",
      "down_interfaces": [
        {
          "name": "Ethernet3",
```

```
          "description": "server_rack_2",
          "status": "down"
        }
      ]
    },
    "bgp_status": {
      "tool": "get_bgp_summary",
      "total_peers": 2,
      "established_peers": 1,
      "non_established_neighbors": [
        {
          "ip": "10.1.2.2",
          "state": "Idle",
          "prefixes": 0
        }
      ]
    }
  }
}
```

The model does not have to invent this record. The application can build it from tool results. Once this kind of record exists, the final answer can be checked before it is shown to the user.

For example, the application could use a simple rule: if `established_peers` is less than `total_peers`, the final answer must mention a BGP issue. That rule does not require a model. It is deterministic validation around the model output.

A simplified check might look like this:

```
def bgp_has_issue(bgp_result: dict)-> bool:
    if "error" in bgp_result:
        return True
    if bgp_result.get("established_peers") != bgp_result.get("total_peers"):
        return True
    for neighbor in bgp_result.get("neighbors", []):
        if neighbor.get("state") != "Established":
            return True
    return False
```

This is the larger pattern we want readers to understand. The model can decide what to inspect and explain what the evidence means, but deterministic code can still check the obvious facts before trusting the final wording.

Checking the answer before trusting it

A tool-using agent has two kinds of output. First, it has the raw tool results. Second, it has the final model response. The final model response should never be treated as more authoritative than the tool results.

If the tool output says one neighbor is `Idle`, but the final answer says all BGP peers are established, the final answer is wrong. The agent sounded confident, but the evidence disagreed. That is exactly the kind of failure production systems must catch.

For the BGP part of this chapter, the answer check can be simple:

- If `established_peers` is lower than `total_peers`, the final answer must report a BGP issue
- If any neighbor state is not `Established`, the final answer must identify that neighbor
- If a neighbor has `prefixes: 0`, the final answer should mention possible route impact
- If `ping_device()` returns `unreachable`, the final answer should not say the target is reachable
- If the tool output contains an error, the final answer should mention the error or ask for another check

These are small checks, but they protect the engineer from a polished answer that ignores the data. They also give you a way to test whether the prompt and agent loop are behaving well.

An answer that passes this check might look like this:

```
Finding:
leaf2 has two issues to investigate. The device is up, but one BGP neighbor is not
established and Ethernet3 is down.

Evidence:
- leaf2 status is up
- Ethernet3 on leaf2 is down
- BGP total_peers is 2
- BGP established_peers is 1
- neighbor 10.1.2.2 is Idle
- neighbor 10.1.2.2 has 0 prefixes
```

```
Likely cause:
Missing routes may be related to the idle BGP neighbor if the route should be
learned through that peer. Ethernet3 may also affect the local server-facing
segment.

Next checks:
Check the peer at 10.1.2.2, inspect BGP logs, verify link state toward spine2,
check Ethernet3 locally, and confirm whether the missing prefix should be
advertised by that peer.
```

This answer does not hide the healthy signals. It says the device is up. It also does not hide the unhealthy signals. It clearly names the idle neighbor, includes the down interface, and explains why prefixes matter.

Designing a structured troubleshooting response

A repeatable answer structure helps both readers and future code. If every troubleshooting answer has a different shape, it becomes harder to review or parse. A small structure gives the agent a better target.

For this chapter, the most useful structure has five parts:

- **Finding**: the short operational conclusion
- **Evidence**: the tool results that support the conclusion
- **Likely cause**: a careful hypothesis, not an unsupported claim
- **Next checks**: what the engineer should verify next
- **Unknowns**: what the agent did not verify

The Unknowns section is especially useful. It keeps the agent honest. If the route table was not checked directly, the answer can say so. If the lab only checked reachability, the answer can say the route itself was not inspected.

A prompt rule for this final format might look like this:

```
Return the final troubleshooting answer using this format:

Finding:
Evidence:
Likely cause:
Next checks:
Unknowns:
```

```
Do not omit unhealthy evidence.
Do not say the network is healthy if a tool result contains an error, Idle peer,
down interface, or unreachable target.
```

This is not just presentation polish. The structure makes it easier for the engineer to scan the answer during an incident. It also makes it easier to compare the final response with the tool results printed above it.

Expanding the missing route investigation

A missing route to host symptom should not immediately be blamed on BGP. The agent should treat it as a symptom and gather supporting evidence. The exact route may be missing because of BGP, static routing, filtering, an access control rule, or a host problem.

In this mocked lab, we can still teach the right habit. The agent can run a reachability check and compare that with BGP and interface evidence. If the target is unreachable, `leaf2` has an idle neighbor with zero prefixes, and `Ethernet3` is down, the agent can say BGP and the server-facing interface are likely areas to investigate next.

The reachability result for an unknown target looks like this:

```
{
  "target": "10.99.99.99",
  "packets_sent": 4,
  "packets_received": 0,
  "packet_loss": 100,
  "status": "unreachable",
  "error": "Destination host unreachable"
}
```

This is not the same as proving a specific route is missing from a routing table. It is a reachability symptom. A careful final answer should say exactly that. It can connect the symptom to the BGP evidence, but it should not claim proof that is not in the tool output.

Table 7.6 compares weak conclusions with stronger, evidence-based conclusions:

Weak conclusion	Evidence-based conclusion
The host is unreachable because BGP is down.	The target is unreachable, and `leaf2` has one idle BGP neighbor with 0 prefixes. If the route should be learned through that peer, BGP is a likely area to investigate. `Ethernet3` is also down and should be checked.
`leaf2` is healthy because the device is up.	`leaf2` is up, but one BGP neighbor is `Idle` and `Ethernet3` is down, so both routing control-plane and local interface state need investigation.
All BGP looks fine.	`leaf2` has `established_peers: 1` out of `total_peers: 2`; neighbor `10.1.2.2` is not established.

Table 7.6: Weak conclusions compared with evidence-based conclusions

This kind of careful wording is what makes an agent useful in network operations. It gives a clear direction without pretending the investigation is complete.

Preparing for reusable tools with MCP

At this point, the tool pattern works inside one Python application. The agent knows about a local tool map, the application executes approved Python functions, and the results return to the model.

That is enough for a lab, but it raises a useful question: what if we want the same network tools to be available outside this one script? What if another assistant, interface, or client should be able to call them without copying the same Python code into every application?

That is where the next chapter starts. We will use Model Context Protocol to package network tools behind a reusable server interface. The idea is the same safety pattern, but with cleaner separation between tools and clients.

Summary

In this chapter, we turned the tool calling mechanics from *Chapter 6* into a practical troubleshooting workflow. The agent used approved mock tools to gather device status, interface state, BGP state, topology context, and reachability evidence.

The main troubleshooting story focused on BGP and missing route to host symptoms. We saw why the agent should not jump to conclusions, why `leaf2` is a useful degraded case, and why an idle BGP neighbor with 0 prefixes and a down local interface should be reported clearly.

We also covered one of the most important production habits early: the final answer must match the tool evidence. If the tool output shows one idle peer, the model should not say all peers are established. Tool results are the evidence, and the final response must respect them.

The chapter kept the workflow mocked and read-only on purpose. That gives every reader a repeatable lab and keeps the focus on the investigation pattern. In the next chapter, we will take the same tool ideas and package them with MCP so network tools can be reused by broader AI assistant integrations.

Get this book's PDF version and more

8

From Lab Agents to Reusable Tools with MCP

In the previous chapter, the troubleshooting agent called Python tools directly. That was the right place to start. The code could map a model-requested tool name to an approved function, execute the function, and return the result to the model. That pattern is useful, but it is still tied to one application.

At some point, useful tools need to move beyond one script. A network team may want the same device status check, BGP summary, interface lookup, or safe show command available to a browser UI, an internal assistant, an editor plugin, or another automation service. Rewriting the same glue code for every client quickly becomes repetitive.

This is where the **Model Context Protocol** (**MCP**) starts to help. MCP gives us a cleaner way to expose tools to clients. The business logic can stay in Python, but the client no longer needs to know exactly how those functions are implemented. It can discover tools, call them through a protocol, and receive structured results.

The goal of this chapter is not to turn MCP into a buzzword. We will keep it practical. We will take the safe mock network tools from the earlier labs, wrap them behind an MCP server, connect a small HTTP bridge, and use a browser interface to test the tools. Read-only first. Always.

In this chapter, we will cover the following topics:

- Reviewing the technical requirements for the MCP lab
- Understanding why direct tool calling does not scale cleanly
- Explaining what MCP adds to the agent workflow
- Reviewing the Lab 5 MCP folder

- Testing the safe network tool wrappers
- Exposing network tools through an MCP server
- Connecting the browser UI through the HTTP bridge
- Running the MCP server and bridge in the correct order
- Testing MCP tools from the browser interface
- Keeping reusable tools safe, read-only, and production-aware

By the end of this chapter, you will understand how the same network tools used by a local agent can be packaged behind a reusable MCP interface. That prepares us for the final chapter, where we look at the production boundaries needed before these patterns touch real infrastructure.

Technical requirements

This chapter uses the Lab 5 MCP files from the Packt repository. The lab stays local, mocked, and read-only. You do not need live network devices, cloud credentials, or a production MCP client to follow the chapter.

You need the following tools and files:

- Python 3.10 or later
- Repository dependencies installed from `requirements.txt`
- The Lab 5 folder at `labs/lab5-mcp/`
- The MCP server at `labs/lab5-mcp/mcp_server.py`
- The HTTP bridge at `labs/lab5-mcp/http_bridge.py`
- The browser UI at `labs/lab5-mcp/ui.html`
- The safe network tool wrappers in `labs/lab5-mcp/network_tools.py`
- The local sanity test at `labs/lab5-mcp/client_test.py`
- The mock network backend at `examples/mock_network_devices.py`

If you followed the earlier setup, the repository should already be cloned and the Python environment should already exist. If not, return to the setup flow in *Chapter 2* before running this lab.

From the repository root, make sure the dependencies are installed with this command:

```
pip install -r requirements.txt
```

Lab 5 uses MCP, Starlette, and Uvicorn for the server and bridge flow. These packages are included in `requirements.txt`, so readers do not need to install them one by one.

Moving beyond direct tool calling

Direct tool calling is a good learning pattern. In *Chapter 6* and *Chapter 7*, the application carried a tool map, the model requested a tool, and the application ran the matching Python function. That kept the flow visible and safe.

The limitation is that the tool contract lives inside one application. If another client needs the same capability, it has to duplicate the integration. A browser UI, a desktop assistant, and an internal automation service should not each need their own version of device lookup and BGP parsing.

MCP helps separate the reusable tool interface from the client. The tool code still belongs to us. The safety checks still belong to us. The difference is that the client can call tools through a standard protocol rather than reaching directly into one local Python class.

Table 8.1 summarizes the shift from direct tool calling to reusable MCP-based tool exposure:

Pattern	How the client gets tools	Best used when
Direct tool calling	One application maps model requests to local Python functions	First labs, prototypes, and simple agents
MCP tool server	A server exposes tools that clients can discover and call	Tools need to be reused by more than one client
HTTP bridge plus UI	A bridge talks to the MCP server and exposes simple HTTP endpoints to a browser	The Lab 5 browser UI needs a visible way to test tools

Table 8.1: Comparing direct tool calling with MCP-based tool reuse

The important point is that MCP does not remove the need for good tool design. It just gives us a cleaner way to expose those tools once they are safe enough to share.

Understanding what MCP adds

Model Context Protocol is a way for clients and servers to exchange tool capabilities and structured results. In practical terms, an MCP server defines the tools it provides, how clients call them, and the shape of the results they receive.

For this book, we do not need to treat MCP as a huge theory topic. We only need to understand what it changes in the workflow. Instead of wiring one agent directly to one set of local functions, we can expose a small network tool server and let clients call those tools in a consistent way.

A useful way to think about MCP is that it creates a contract between tool providers and tool users. The provider owns the implementation and safety checks. The client discovers and calls the tool. The result comes back as structured data.

> **Note**
>
> This chapter assumes familiarity with devices, interfaces, BGP, `ping`, and `show` commands. Newer terms include `stdio`, SSE, MCP server, MCP client, transport, and HTTP bridge. We will explain these only as needed for the Lab 5 workflow.

Figure 8.1 shows the difference between direct tool calling and the MCP-based pattern:

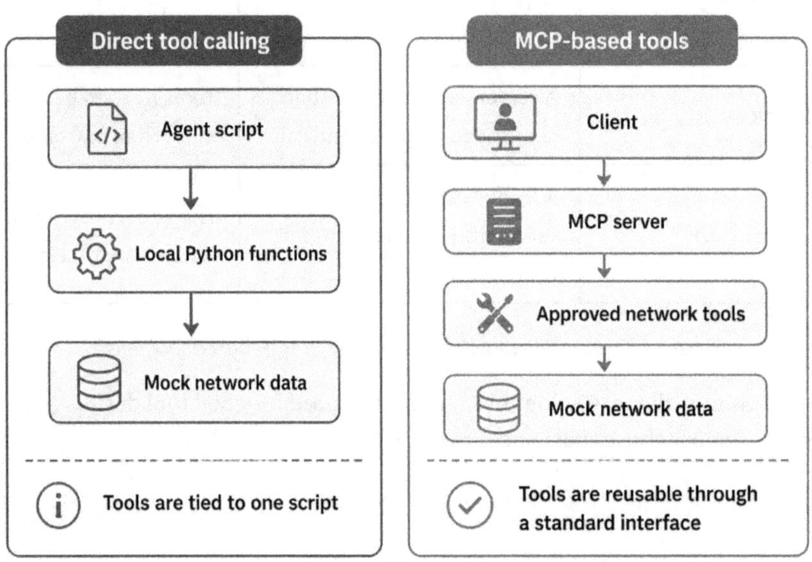

Figure 8.1: Direct tool calling compared with MCP-based reusable tools

The figure should look familiar. We are not replacing the safe tool ideas from the previous chapters. We are moving them behind an interface that can be reused by more than one client.

Reviewing the Lab 5 architecture

The Lab 5 folder contains a small but useful architecture. It keeps business logic, MCP exposure, HTTP bridging, and the browser interface in separate files. That separation is the point of the lab.

The request path looks like this:

```
ui.html -> http_bridge.py -> mcp_server.py -> network_tools.py ->
mock_network_devices.py
```

The browser does not call the mock network functions directly. It talks to the HTTP bridge. The bridge acts as an MCP client and calls the MCP server. The MCP server exposes the approved network tools. The tool wrappers call the mock backend.

Figure 8.2 shows this request flow in the Lab 5 implementation:

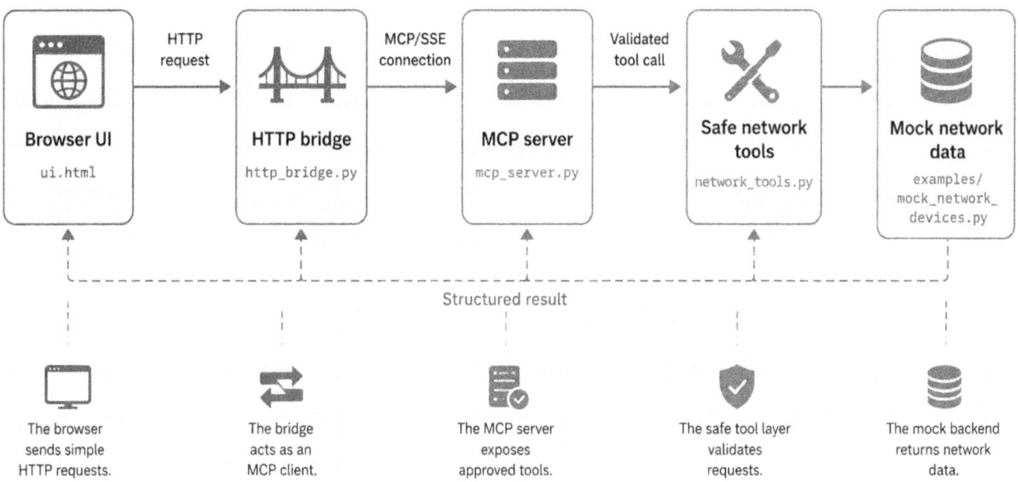

Figure 8.2: Lab 5 MCP architecture and request flow

This layout may look like more moving parts than a single Python script, and it is. That is the trade-off. We add a little structure so the tools can be reused and tested through cleaner boundaries.

Table 8.2 lists the main files in the Lab 5 folder and explains what readers should focus on in each file:

File	What it does	Reader focus
`network_tools.py`	Wraps the mock network functions with safe checks	Understand where validation and read-only boundaries live
`mcp_server.py`	Exposes safe network wrappers as MCP tools	Understand the reusable tool interface
`http_bridge.py`	Connects to the MCP server and exposes HTTP endpoints	Understand how the browser reaches the MCP tools
`ui.html`	Provides a browser interface for calling the tools	Test the workflow visually
`client_test.py`	Runs local sanity checks against the tool wrappers	Debug tool logic before starting MCP

Table 8.2: Lab 5 files and reader focus

This is a good pattern to keep in mind. When a tool layer gets hard to reason about, separate the business logic from the transport. That makes both easier to test.

Reviewing the safe network tool wrappers

The file `network_tools.py` is where the lab keeps the safety checks close to the tool logic. The MCP server imports these wrappers and exposes them to clients, but the wrappers decide what is allowed.

The wrappers call the same mock backend we used in earlier chapters. That means Lab 5 builds on the known topology instead of introducing a second model of the network. The tool layer still returns structured dictionaries, which makes the output easier to inspect, log, and pass to another system.

Table 8.3 summarizes the safe wrapper functions that sit between MCP and the mock network backend:

Wrapper function	Purpose	Safety check
`list_devices()`	Returns devices in the mock topology	No arguments and no live access
`safe_device_status(device)`	Returns status for one known device	Rejects unknown devices
`safe_interface_status(device, interface=None)`	Returns one interface or all interfaces for a device	Validates the device before lookup
`safe_bgp_summary(device)`	Returns BGP peer state for a device	Validates the device before lookup
`safe_ping(target, count=4)`	Runs a mock reachability check	Limits count between 1 and 10
`safe_show_command(device, command)`	Runs approved read-only `show` commands	Blocks commands that do not start with `show`
`safe_topology_info()`	Returns the mock topology map	Static read-only data

Table 8.3: Safe network wrappers used by the MCP server

The wrappers are intentionally boring. That is a compliment. The best network tools for agents are narrow, predictable, and easy to reject when the input is wrong.

Testing the tool layer before MCP

Before starting the MCP server, test the business logic directly. This is a useful habit because it separates tool bugs from protocol or bridge issues. If the local wrapper test fails, MCP is not the first thing to debug.

Run the local sanity test from the repository root:

```
python3 labs/lab5-mcp/client_test.py
```

A successful run should show several tool checks. The following shortened output shows the most important parts:

```
======================================================================
Available devices
======================================================================
{
  "source": "mock_network_devices",
  "devices": ["spine1", "spine2", "leaf1", "leaf2"]
}

======================================================================
BGP summary: leaf2
======================================================================
{
  "device": "leaf2",
  "total_peers": 2,
  "established_peers": 1,
  "neighbors": [
    {"ip": "10.1.1.2", "state": "Established", "prefixes": 50},
    {"ip": "10.1.2.2", "state": "Idle", "prefixes": 0}
  ]
}

======================================================================
Interface status: leaf2 Ethernet3
======================================================================
{
  "device": "leaf2",
  "interface": "Ethernet3",
  "description": "server_rack_2",
  "status": "down",
  "speed": "1G"
}

======================================================================
Blocked unsafe command
======================================================================
{
  "error": "Only read-only show commands are allowed in this lab",
  "blocked_command": "configure terminal",
```

```
    "example": "show ip bgp summary"
  }
```

This test confirms two things. First, the wrapper layer can read useful mock network data. Second, the unsafe command path is blocked before any unsafe request is accepted by the tool layer.

Exposing network tools through the MCP server

The file `mcp_server.py` turns the safe wrappers into MCP tools. It uses `FastMCP` and registers Python functions with the `@mcp.tool()` decorator. Each decorated function becomes a tool that an MCP client can discover and call.

A shortened example from the server looks like this:

```
from mcp.server.fastmcp import FastMCP

mcp = FastMCP("network-agent-tools")

@mcp.tool()
def bgp_summary(device: str)-> dict:
    """Get BGP neighbor summary for a lab network device."""
    return safe_bgp_summary(device)
```

The tool name exposed through MCP is `bgp_summary`, while the internal wrapper is `safe_bgp_summary()`. That is a useful separation. The public tool can have a simple name, while the implementation can keep the safety behavior explicit.

Table 8.4 lists the MCP tools exposed by the Lab 5 server and the wrapper each one calls:

MCP tool	**Internal wrapper**	**What readers can test**
`devices`	`list_devices()`	List the devices available in the mock topology
`device_status`	`safe_device_status()`	Return operational status for one device
`interface_status`	`safe_interface_status()`	Return one interface or all interfaces for a device

MCP tool	Internal wrapper	What readers can test
`bgp_summary`	`safe_bgp_summary()`	Return BGP neighbor state for a device
`ping`	`safe_ping()`	Run a mock reachability check
`show_command`	`safe_show_command()`	Run an allowed read-only show command
`topology`	`safe_topology_info()`	Return the spine-leaf topology map

Table 8.4: MCP tools exposed by the Lab 5 server

Notice that the tool names are not the same as the earlier Lab 4 function names. That is okay. What matters is that the tool names are clear, the inputs are narrow, and the outputs are structured.

Running the MCP server

The server can run in two modes. Without flags, it uses `stdio` mode for MCP-capable clients. For the browser UI in this chapter, we use Server-Sent Events (SSE) mode so the HTTP bridge can connect to it.

Start the MCP server first:

```
python3 labs/lab5-mcp/mcp_server.py --sse
```

The server should start in SSE mode and listen on `http://localhost:8000`:

```
Starting MCP server in sse mode...
  Listening on http://localhost:8000
  Start the bridge next: python3 labs/lab5-mcp/http_bridge.py
```

Keep this terminal open. If you close the server, the bridge will not be able to connect, and the browser UI will return connection errors.

Tip

If the server fails to start, check that `mcp` is installed through `requirements.txt` and that you are running the command from the repository root.

Connecting the HTTP bridge

The browser UI does not call the MCP server directly. Instead, `http_bridge.py` acts as an MCP client and exposes simple HTTP endpoints for the browser. This is why the bridge sits between the UI and the MCP server.

The bridge connects to the MCP server at this address:

```
MCP_SERVER_URL = "http://localhost:8000/sse"
```

It then exposes HTTP routes such as `/devices`, `/status`, `/bgp`, `/interface`, `/ping`, `/command`, and `/topology` on port 8765.

Start the bridge in a second terminal:

```
python3 labs/lab5-mcp/http_bridge.py
```

A successful bridge startup should show that it connected to the MCP server and registered the available tools:

```
============================================================
  Lab 5 — HTTP → MCP Bridge
============================================================
  MCP server:  http://localhost:8000/sse
  Bridge HTTP: http://localhost:8765
============================================================

🔌 Connecting to MCP server at http://localhost:8000/sse ...
  Tools registered: ['devices', 'device_status', 'interface_status',
'bgp_summary', 'ping', 'show_command', 'topology']
☑ MCP session established
🌐 Bridge HTTP on http://localhost:8765
   Open labs/lab5-mcp/ui.html in your browser
```

This output is useful because it confirms that the bridge is not just running as a web server; it has also connected to the MCP server and can see the registered tools.

Opening the browser UI

With the MCP server and bridge running, open the UI file in your browser. On macOS, you can use the following command from the repository root:

```
open labs/lab5-mcp/ui.html
```

On other systems, you can open the file manually in a browser or double-click `ui.html` from the file explorer.

The UI is intentionally simple. It gives you buttons and inputs for device status, BGP summary, interface status, ping, show command, device listing, and topology. When you click a tool, the browser calls the bridge, the bridge calls the MCP server, and the MCP server runs the safe wrapper.

Table 8.5 maps browser actions to example bridge calls and MCP tools:

Browser action	**Example bridge call**	**MCP tool**
List devices	`/devices`	`devices`
Device Status	`/status?device=spine1`	`device_status`
BGP Summary	`/bgp?device=leaf2`	`bgp_summary`
Get Interface	`/interface?device=leaf2&interface=Ethernet3`	`interface_status`
Ping	`/ping?target=10.99.99.99&count=4`	`ping`
Run Command	`/command?device=spine1&command=show%20ip%20bgp%20summary`	`show_command`

Browser action	Example bridge call	MCP tool
View Topology	`/topology`	`topology`

Table 8.5: Browser actions, example bridge calls, and MCP tools

This mapping is the reason the bridge is helpful. The browser only needs simple HTTP calls, while the bridge handles the MCP session and tool invocation behind the scenes.

Testing the MCP tools from the UI

Start with a safe and obvious test. Select `spine1` and click **Device Status**. The response should show that `spine1` is up, running `cEOS`, and acting as a spine switch.

Next, select `leaf2` and click **BGP Summary**. This is the useful degraded case from earlier chapters. The response should show that `leaf2` has two BGP peers, but only one is established. Neighbor `10.1.2.2` is in the `Idle` state with 0 prefixes.

Then test the interface tool by selecting `leaf2` and entering `Ethernet3`. The result should show that `Ethernet3` is down and has the description `server_rack_2`.

Finally, test the show command boundary. Run the allowed command first:

```
show ip bgp summary
```

Then try a command that should be blocked:

```
configure terminal
```

The blocked command should return an error, not execute. That is exactly what we want. The point of the lab is not just that tools can be exposed. The point is that safe tools can be exposed with clear boundaries.

Understanding why the bridge exists

At first, the bridge may seem like extra plumbing. Why not have the browser call the MCP server directly? The short answer is that browsers are easiest to work with through simple HTTP and JSON calls, while the MCP server uses MCP over SSE in this lab.

The bridge plays two roles. First, it acts as an MCP client. It connects to the MCP server, initializes a session, and discovers the available tools. Second, it exposes normal HTTP routes that the browser can call.

The simplified bridge pattern looks like this:

```
async def handle_bgp(request: Request)-> JSONResponse:
    device = request.query_params.get("device", "")
    return JSONResponse(
        await call_tool("bgp_summary", {"device": device})
    )
```

That small route tells the whole story. The browser sends a device name to the bridge. The bridge calls the MCP tool named `bgp_summary`. The result comes back as JSON that the browser can render.

This is also why the bridge is useful for troubleshooting. If the UI fails, you can test whether the bridge is running. If the bridge fails, you can test whether the MCP server is running. If the MCP server fails, you can test the tool wrappers with `client_test.py`.

Running the lab in the correct order

Order matters in this lab. The bridge expects the MCP server to be available. The UI expects the bridge to be available. Start them in the wrong order and you will get connection errors that look more confusing than they are.

Run the Lab 5 MCP workflow in this order:

1. First, test the safe wrapper layer:

   ```
   python3 labs/lab5-mcp/client_test.py
   ```

   Confirm that the tool wrappers return mock network data and block unsafe commands.

2. Next, start the MCP server:

   ```
   python3 labs/lab5-mcp/mcp_server.py --sse
   ```

   Confirm that the server starts on `http://localhost:8000`.

3. Then, start the HTTP bridge in a second terminal:

```
python3 labs/lab5-mcp/http_bridge.py
```

Confirm that the bridge connects to the MCP server and exposes `http://localhost:8765`.

4. Finally, open the browser UI:

```
open labs/lab5-mcp/ui.html
```

Confirm that the browser UI can call the tools through the bridge.

If something fails, work backward through the chain. First check the wrapper test, then the MCP server, then the bridge, and finally the UI.

Troubleshooting the MCP lab

Most Lab 5 issues are startup or dependency issues. The tools themselves are small. The moving parts are the server process, the bridge process, and the browser.

Table 8.6 lists common MCP lab symptoms and the first checks to try:

Symptom	**Likely cause**	**First check**
Bridge cannot connect to MCP server	MCP server is not running in SSE mode	Start `mcp_server.py` with `--sse` before starting `http_bridge.py`
Browser shows connection failure	HTTP bridge is not running	Confirm `http://localhost:8765` is available
Tool returns unknown device	Device name is not in the mock topology	Use `spine1`, `spine2`, `leaf1`, or `leaf2`
Unsafe command returns an error	Command does not start with `show`	Use a read-only command such as `show ip bgp summary`

Symptom	Likely cause	First check
Import error for MCP or Starlette	Dependencies are missing	Run `pip install -r requirements.txt`
UI opens but no data appears	Bridge or MCP server is down	Restart the run order from step 2

Table 8.6: Common MCP lab symptoms and first troubleshooting checks

Troubleshooting this lab is a good reminder that distributed workflows fail in layers. The trick is to test each layer separately instead of changing everything at once.

Keeping MCP tools safe

MCP makes tools easier to expose, which means safety matters even more. A tool that is safe inside one local script can become risky if it is exposed to multiple clients without the same boundaries.

The Lab 5 tool layer keeps the safety boundaries intentionally simple:

- Only known mock devices are accepted
- Unknown devices return structured errors
- Ping count is limited
- Only read-only show commands are allowed
- Configuration commands are blocked
- Tool results are returned as structured dictionaries
- No credentials or live devices are used

Table 8.7 maps the Lab 5 safety controls to the risks they reduce:

Safety control	Implemented in	Why it matters
Known device validation	`validate_device()`	Prevents tools from acting on unknown targets
Read-only command allowlist	`safe_show_command()`	Blocks configuration mode commands

Safety control	Implemented in	Why it matters
Ping count limit	`safe_ping()`	Prevents excessive simulated requests
Structured error payloads	All safe wrappers	Keeps failures visible to callers
Mock network backend	`mock_network_devices.py`	Makes the lab repeatable and safe
Separate bridge and server	`http_bridge.py` and `mcp_server.py`	Makes the request path easier to debug

Table 8.7: Safety controls in the Lab 5 MCP tool layer

The safety lesson is the same one we have used throughout the book. Tools should be narrow, observable, and boring. MCP does not change that. It only makes the tool boundary more reusable.

Deciding when MCP is useful

MCP is useful when the tool should live beyond one application. It is not automatically required for every script. If you are building a small local experiment, direct tool calling may be simpler. If you are packaging tools for multiple assistants or clients, MCP starts to make sense.

Use this practical rule when deciding whether to add MCP:

- Use direct tool calling for one script, quick debugging, or the earliest lab prototype
- Use an MCP server when multiple clients need the same tool interface
- Use the HTTP bridge and UI when a browser needs to test tools through simple HTTP calls
- Add production controls before connecting any MCP tool to real devices

Do not add MCP because it sounds advanced. Add it when it gives you a cleaner tool contract, better reuse, and a safer path for multiple clients to call the same tools.

Comparing MCP transport choices

The Lab 5 server can run in more than one transport mode. This matters because different clients expect different connection styles. A local desktop assistant may use `stdio`, while the browser flow in this chapter uses SSE through the HTTP bridge.

You do not need to master every MCP transport detail to complete the lab. What matters is knowing which mode you are using and why. The browser UI path needs the MCP server in SSE mode because the bridge connects to the server over a local URL.

The lab uses three connection patterns:

- Use `stdio` when a local MCP client starts the server process and exchanges messages through standard input and output
- Use SSE when the bridge connects to a running MCP server over `http://localhost:8000/sse`
- Use the HTTP bridge when a browser needs endpoints such as `/bgp` and the bridge should call MCP behind the scenes

The practical rule is simple: use `stdio` for direct MCP clients, use SSE when another process needs to connect to a running MCP server, and use the HTTP bridge when a browser needs to test the tools.

Designing stable MCP tool contracts

Once a tool is exposed through MCP, its name, arguments, and return shape become a contract. Other clients may start depending on that contract. Changing it casually can break the UI, an assistant, or another internal workflow.

A good MCP tool contract should make three things clear:

- What the tool does
- Which arguments it accepts
- What shape the result returns

The Lab 5 tools follow that pattern. For example, the public MCP tool is named `bgp_summary`, and it accepts a `device` argument. The internal wrapper can change later, but the public tool contract should remain stable unless we intentionally version the change.

Before exposing a tool through MCP, use this simple contract checklist:

- Use a short tool name, such as `bgp_summary`
- Make required arguments clear, such as `device` for `bgp_summary`
- Use safe defaults and limits for optional arguments, such as `count` in `ping`
- Return structured dictionaries with predictable keys
- Return structured error data instead of crashing
- Keep safety checks in the wrapper layer before execution

This contract mindset keeps the tool layer maintainable. It also helps readers understand that MCP is not only a way to run tools; it is a way to publish a clear interface to those tools.

Avoiding common MCP design mistakes

MCP can make tools easier to expose, but it can also make bad tool design spread faster. If a vague or unsafe tool is published through MCP, every client that discovers it inherits that problem.

The most common mistake is exposing tools that are too broad. A tool named `run_command` sounds convenient, but it creates risk unless the allowed commands, devices, and arguments are tightly controlled. Lab 5 keeps this safer by exposing `show_command` and blocking anything that does not start with `show`.

Another mistake is hiding errors. If a device name is wrong, the wrapper should return a structured error with the available devices. That is more useful than a stack trace and safer than a silent failure.

A third mistake is mixing business logic with transport logic. The MCP server should not become the place where all network behavior lives. The server should expose tools. The wrapper layer should handle validation and business rules. The backend should provide the data source.

When the MCP tool layer grows, use these safer patterns:

- Avoid broad tools such as `run_command()`. Expose narrow tools with explicit arguments instead.
- Avoid silent failures. Return structured error dictionaries that clients can inspect.
- Avoid mixing transport and business logic. Keep validation in `network_tools.py`; keep server and bridge transport code separate.
- Avoid unbounded arguments. Validate values before tool execution.
- Avoid missing audit data. In production, log tool name, arguments, result status, and duration.

These are small design choices in a lab, but they become major reliability choices in production. The more reusable the tool becomes, the more careful the contract needs to be.

Checking production reality

Lab 5 is still a mock lab. That is intentional. We are using MCP to learn the tool packaging pattern, not to claim that a browser UI and local bridge are production-ready.

A production MCP deployment would need more controls. The tool server would need authentication, authorization, structured logging, request IDs, rate limits, timeout policies, input schemas, secrets management, and clear ownership. The bridge would need to run as a managed service rather than a local process started from a terminal.

The tool contract would also need careful review. Which users can call which tools? Which devices are in scope? Which commands are allowed? How are errors logged? How are approvals handled if a future tool changes state? Those questions are not optional once a tool touches real infrastructure.

Table 8.8 summarizes the production concerns we will carry into the next chapter:

Production concern	Why it matters	Chapter 9 direction
Authentication	Clients should not call tools anonymously	Identify users and clients before tool access
Authorization	Not every user should call every tool	Use role-based access control and allowlists
Logging	Tool calls need an audit trail	Log user, tool, arguments, result status, and duration
Secrets management	Credentials should not live in code	Use environment variables or secrets managers
Observability	Failures need to be visible	Track errors, latency, tool usage, and success rates
Approvals	Write actions require human control	Keep read-only first and require approval for changes
Validation	Tool input and output must be checked	Use schemas, typed models, and deterministic checks

Table 8.8: Production concerns that remain after the MCP lab

This chapter gives us the reusable tool interface. The next chapter is where we put production expectations around that interface.

Reviewing what we built

Before we close the chapter, it is worth stepping back and looking at the complete Lab 5 path. We did not build a full production agent. We built a reusable and testable way to expose network tools.

The finished lab has four layers:

- The mock network backend in `examples/mock_network_devices.py`
- The safe wrapper layer in `labs/lab5-mcp/network_tools.py`
- The MCP server in `labs/lab5-mcp/mcp_server.py`
- The HTTP bridge and browser UI in `labs/lab5-mcp/http_bridge.py` and `labs/lab5-mcp/ui.html`

That layering is the real takeaway. If we later replace the mock backend with a real network backend, the MCP server should not have to change much. The wrapper layer is where validation and safety should grow.

Summary

In this chapter, we moved from direct tool calling to reusable MCP tooling. The key idea is simple: the same network tools that helped a local agent can be exposed through an MCP server so other clients can discover and call them.

We reviewed the Lab 5 architecture, tested the safe network wrappers, exposed those wrappers through `mcp_server.py`, connected the browser UI through `http_bridge.py`, and tested device, BGP, interface, ping, show command, and topology tools from the UI.

We also kept the safety line clear. MCP makes tools easier to reuse, but it does not make unsafe tools safe. The lab stays read-only, uses mock data, validates known devices, blocks configuration commands, and returns structured errors.

In the next chapter, we will move from reusable lab tools to production readiness and review the checklists, guardrails, logging, approvals, secrets, observability, and operational boundaries needed before a network agent can be evaluated in a real environment.

Join us on Discord

For discussions around the book and to connect with your peers, join us on Discord at `packt.link/discordcloud` or scan the QR code below:

9

Moving Toward Production-Ready Network Agents

A lab agent can be impressive. It can call a tool, inspect a BGP neighbor, summarize a fault, and make the workflow feel much faster than manual investigation. That is useful, but it is still not production-ready.

Production is where the questions change. Instead of asking whether the agent can answer a prompt, we ask whether the system can be trusted when a device is unreachable, a credential expires, a tool returns partial data, or a user asks for an unsafe command. The agent is only one part of that system.

In the previous chapter, we exposed reusable network tools through **Model Context Protocol** (**MCP**). That gave us a cleaner tool interface, but a reusable interface is not automatically a safe operational interface. Once a tool can be called by more than one client, the boundaries around that tool become more important.

This chapter is the production reality check for the whole book. We will not pretend that the lab repository is a complete production platform. Instead, we will use the Lab 6 production-readiness files as supporting patterns and build a practical checklist for moving from a local demo toward a controlled, observable, read-only-first operational prototype.

In this chapter, we will cover the following topics:

- Reviewing the technical requirements for production readiness
- Understanding why production is different from a lab
- Defining the production boundary for a network agent
- Keeping the first operational step read-only
- Deciding what should not be automated

- Applying authentication, authorization, and secrets handling
- Validating tool inputs and outputs before trusting them
- Adding approval gates for risky actions
- Logging, auditing, and observing agent behavior
- Using Lab 6 as a production-readiness reference pattern
- Planning a staged rollout from lab to controlled evaluation

By the end of this chapter, you should have a clear checklist for evaluating whether a network agent is ready to move beyond local labs. More importantly, you should know which questions to ask before connecting any agent workflow to real infrastructure.

Technical requirements

This chapter uses the production-readiness examples from the Packt repository. The examples stay local, mocked, and read-only. You do not need live devices, production credentials, or an enterprise deployment platform to follow the chapter.

You need the following tools and files:

- Python 3.10 or later
- Repository dependencies in `requirements.txt`
- Lab 6 production-readiness files in `labs/lab6-production-readiness/`
- Mock network backend in `examples/mock_network_devices.py`

From the repository root, make sure the Python environment has the project dependencies installed:

```
pip install -r requirements.txt
```

The two runnable Lab 6 examples can be run with the following commands:

```
python3 labs/lab6-production-readiness/safe_tools.py
python3 labs/lab6-production-readiness/production_agent_skeleton.py
```

> **Note**
>
> `labs/lab6-production-readiness/` is a reference pattern, not a complete production deployment. The point is to show the guardrail layer that should sit around agent tools before those tools touch real infrastructure.

With the requirements in place, we can step back from the lab and define what production readiness actually means for a network agent.

Understanding why production is different from a lab

A lab is designed to be friendly. The inputs are known, the devices are mocked, the credentials are not real, and failure is cheap. Production is different. In production, the wrong command, the wrong target, or the wrong summary can waste time during an incident or create a real outage.

That does not mean network agents should never be used in real environments. It means the first production milestone should be a controlled, read-only prototype with strong visibility. The goal is to learn how the agent behaves under real operational conditions without giving it permission to change the network.

A production-minded design must answer questions that a lab demo can ignore. Who called the tool? Which device was targeted? Was the command allowed? What evidence did the agent use? Did the system fail closed? Can another engineer replay the decision later?

Table 9.1 compares the assumptions that are acceptable in a lab with the controls expected before production use:

Area	Lab assumption	Production expectation
Network backend	Mock devices return predictable data	Real backends need timeouts, retries, and failure handling
Tool access	Any lab user can run the demo	Users and clients must be authenticated and authorized
Commands	Only safe examples are shown	Commands must be allowlisted and logged
Data quality	Mock output is known in advance	Tool output must be validated and labeled
Failures	A failed demo can be restarted	Failures must be visible, bounded, and auditable
Changes	No configuration changes are allowed	Any write action needs approval, evidence, and rollback planning

Table 9.1: Lab readiness compared with production readiness

The table should not discourage experimentation. It should keep the transition honest. A working demo is valuable, but production readiness begins when the workflow can be controlled, observed, and reviewed by someone other than the person who built it.

Defining the production boundary

Before we discuss individual controls, we need to define the boundary of the system. A network agent is not only the model. It includes the user or client, the agent application, the tool server, the approved tools, the network backend, and the logging and approval layers around them.

This boundary matters because safety does not belong in one place. The prompt can guide behavior, but code must enforce policy. The tool can reject bad inputs, but the system still needs authorization. The model can summarize evidence, but logs must preserve what actually happened.

The production boundary we care about is shown in *Figure 9.1*:

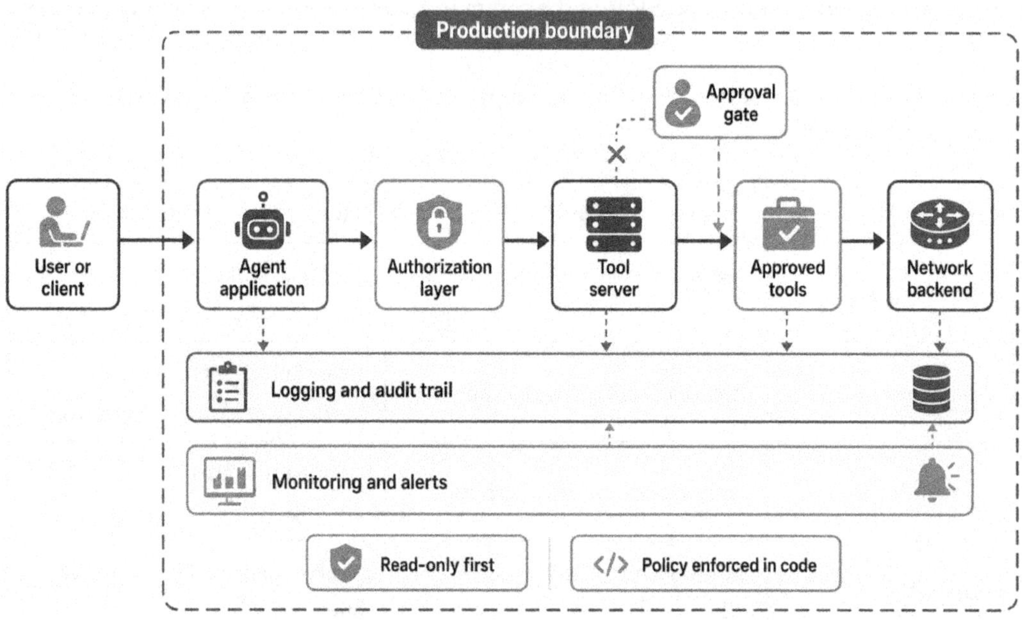

Figure 9.1: Production boundary for a network agent

The important idea is separation of responsibility. The model can reason over evidence, but the application owns execution. The tool layer owns validation. The authorization layer owns access. The logging layer owns traceability. When those responsibilities are separated, the system becomes easier to review and safer to operate.

Keeping the first operational step read-only

The safest first step outside the lab is read-only operation. A read-only agent can still provide meaningful value. It can enrich alerts, summarize BGP state, inspect interface status, check route visibility, and prepare a clean handoff for an engineer.

Read-only does not mean risk-free. A read-only tool can still leak information, overload a device, or produce a misleading summary. But the blast radius is much smaller than a tool that can change configuration. That makes read-only workflows the right first milestone.

Common read-only tools include the following:

- `device_status` for inventory and health data
- `interface_status` for interface state and descriptions
- `bgp_summary` for peer state and prefix counts
- `topology` for device relationships
- `show_command` for approved show commands
- `ping` or reachability checks with bounded counts
- Log lookup tools that return filtered events rather than raw unlimited logs

Read-only tools give the team a way to evaluate usefulness before deciding whether any recommendation or action should become more automated. That evaluation period is where many production problems can be found safely.

Deciding what should not be automated

A useful production plan also says what the agent should not do. This is not negative thinking. It is scope control. If the team cannot explain why a capability is safe, observable, and recoverable, it should not be automated yet.

The most dangerous tools are usually the broad ones. A tool named `run_command()` sounds flexible, but flexibility is exactly what makes it risky. A safer design exposes narrow tools that describe their purpose and validate their inputs before doing anything.

Table 9.2 gives a practical way to separate safer read-only tools from higher-risk tools:

Tool or capability	Risk level	Recommended production stance
`device_status(device)`	Low	Allow after authentication and device allowlist validation
`bgp_summary(device)`	Low	Allow for approved devices and log every call
`show_command(device, command)`	Medium	Allow only approved read-only show commands
`run_command(device, command)`	High	Avoid broad command execution; replace with narrower tools
Configuration change tools	High	Require approval, ticket reference, diff, and rollback plan
Restart or clear-session tools	High	Keep out of the first production phase unless tightly controlled

Table 9.2: Read-only tools and higher-risk capabilities

The safest design is usually boring. Make tools specific. Make arguments narrow. Make unsafe actions impossible by default. That gives the agent less room to surprise you.

Applying authentication and authorization

Once a tool can be called outside one local script, the system needs to know who or what is calling it. *Authentication* proves identity. *Authorization* decides what that identity can do.

Network teams already think this way for devices and change systems. Agents should not be different. A junior operator, an on-call engineer, an automation service account, and an administrator should not automatically have the same tool access.

A simple **role-based access control** (**RBAC**) model might look like the one in *Table 9.3*:

Role	**Allowed tools**	**Blocked actions**
Viewer	Read-only status, topology, and summaries	Any command execution, approvals, or changes
Network operator	Approved read-only tools and approved show commands	Configuration changes and broad command tools
Senior engineer	Read-only tools, approved diagnostics, and approval review	Unreviewed write actions
Automation maintainer	Tool tests, wrapper updates, and lab validation	Production execution without change control
Administrator	Policy and access management	Bypassing audit, approval, or logging requirements

Table 9.3: Example role-based tool access

The exact roles will differ by organization. The important part is that the tool layer should not treat every caller the same. Access should match responsibility, and every access decision should be reviewable later.

Handling secrets and credentials

Secrets are where many automation projects become risky. A production agent should never receive credentials through a prompt. Credentials should not be hard-coded in Python files, committed to GitHub, printed in logs, or echoed back in model output.

The preferred pattern is to keep credentials outside the code. Use environment variables, a secrets manager, or a platform-specific credential store. Use service accounts with the least-privilege access needed for the tool. Start with read-only credentials before any account is allowed to change state.

For this book, the labs stay mocked, which is exactly why they are safe to run. In production, secrets handling becomes part of the architecture, not an afterthought. The tool should receive a credential reference or session from a trusted runtime, not ask the model what password to use.

A simple secrets policy for network agents should include these rules:

- Do not place usernames, passwords, tokens, or keys in prompts
- Do not commit secrets to the repository
- Do not print secrets in terminal output or logs
- Use read-only service accounts for the first operational phase
- Rotate credentials and document ownership
- Separate lab credentials from production credentials
- Treat model outputs as visible to operators and logs unless explicitly designed otherwise

Secrets management is not exciting, but it is one of the first things reviewers will ask about. If the answer is unclear, the agent should stay in the lab.

Validating inputs and outputs

The validation lessons from earlier chapters become more important in production. The model may request a tool, but the tool layer should decide whether the request is valid. The tool may return data, but the agent should not blindly summarize it as truth without checking the shape and meaning.

Input validation protects the network from bad requests. Output validation protects the operator from bad conclusions. Both are required.

Table 9.4 summarizes validation checks that should exist around production-minded network tools:

Validation point	What to check	Example
Device input	Device exists and is in the approved scope	Reject `core99` if it is not in the allowlist
Command input	Command is read-only and allowlisted	Allow `show ip bgp summary`; block `configure terminal`
Argument limits	Counts, timeouts, and sizes are bounded	Limit count for `ping` and apply request timeouts
Tool output shape	Required keys and data types exist	Check `total_peers`, `established_peers`, and `neighbors`

Validation point	What to check	Example
Error payloads	Failures return structured errors	Return `allowed: false` with a reason instead of a stack trace
Agent conclusion	Summary matches tool evidence	Do not say all BGP peers are healthy if one peer is `Idle`

Table 9.4: Input and output validation checks for network tools

Validation should feel repetitive. That is the point. A production tool should reject bad input every time, not only when the demo path happens to be clean.

Using the Lab 6 safety wrapper demo

The safety wrapper demo is `safe_tools.py` in `labs/lab6-production-readiness/`. It demonstrates a small guardrail layer around the mock network tools. It is not an enterprise policy engine. It is a readable example of where policy and audit logging can live.

Run the demo from the repository root:

```
python3 labs/lab6-production-readiness/safe_tools.py
```

A full run shows allowed read-only calls, blocked unsafe calls, blocked unknown devices, and audit events. The following shortened excerpt shows the allowed BGP summary and blocked unsafe command path:

```
☑ Allowed BGP summary
{
  "device": "leaf2",
  "total_peers": 2,
  "established_peers": 1,
  "neighbors": [
    {"ip": "10.1.1.2", "state": "Established", "prefixes": 50},
    {"ip": "10.1.2.2", "state": "Idle", "prefixes": 0}
  ]
}

⊘ Blocked unsafe command
{
```

```
  "error": "configuration and exec commands are blocked; only read-only show
commands are allowed",
  "allowed": false,
  "risk": "high",
  "requires_approval": true
}
```

This is the behavior we want from a guardrail layer. The tool allows safe observation, blocks unsafe commands, and returns a structured reason instead of failing silently.

Designing tool safety and approval workflows

Not every tool should follow the same approval path. Read-only tools may be allowed automatically for approved users. Risky tools should require human review before execution. Configuration-changing tools should require even more context: a ticket, a proposed diff, expected impact, and rollback notes.

A useful approval workflow does not simply ask a human to click **Approve**. It gives the human enough evidence to make a decision. The request should include the exact target, the exact action, the reason, the evidence, the expected result, and the risk level.

A production approval flow is shown in *Figure 9.2*:

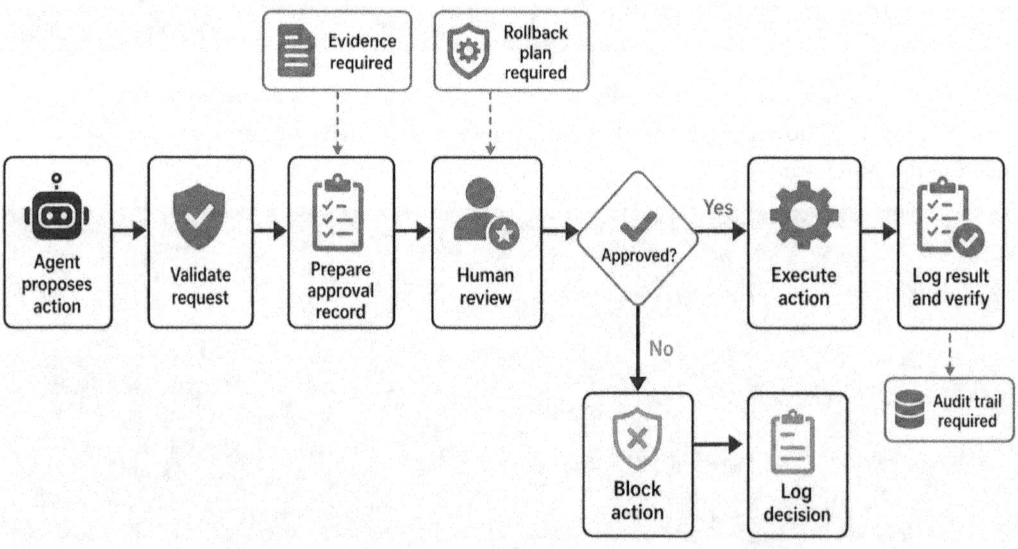

Figure 9.2: Human approval flow for network-changing actions

The approval gate is what separates recommendation from execution. The agent may propose a next step, but the system should decide whether that step is allowed automatically, requires approval, or must be blocked entirely.

Logging every tool call

A production agent should leave a trail. If it calls `bgp_summary` for `leaf2`, blocks `configure terminal`, or returns an error for an unknown device, that event should be logged in a structured form.

Logging is not only for debugging. It is also how the team builds trust. An engineer should be able to ask what the agent checked, when it checked it, what the result was, and why the final answer said what it said.

For production use, each tool call should include fields like the ones in *Table 9.5*. The Lab 6 demo shows a smaller in-memory version of this audit pattern, while a real deployment should add identity, timing, and approval fields as needed:

Log field	**Why it matters**	**Example value**
`timestamp`	Shows when the call happened	`2026-06-28T18:36:38Z`
user or `client_id`	Identifies who or what called the tool	`noc-operator-1`
`tool`	Shows which capability was used	`bgp_summary`
`device`	Shows the target	`leaf2`
`command`	Records the command when applicable	`show ip bgp summary`
`decision.allowed`	Shows whether policy allowed execution	`true` or `false`
`decision.reason`	Explains the policy result	`read-only command approved`
`result_summary`	Summarizes outcome	`success`, `blocked`, or `timeout`

Log field	Why it matters	Example value
`duration_ms`	Supports latency monitoring	`184`
`approval_id`	Links risky actions to approval records	`CHG-20491`

Table 9.5: Recommended tool call logging fields

The log should not include secrets or full raw payloads by default. Store enough to audit the action, but do not create a second place where sensitive data can leak.

Reviewing an audit event

The Lab 6 safety wrapper records audit events in memory. In a real system, those events would go to a durable log destination, such as a log pipeline, a security information and event management (SIEM) platform, a database, or an incident record.

The simplified event below shows the core decision record from the Lab 6 demo:

```
{
  "timestamp": "2026-06-28T18:36:38.320934+00:00",
  "tool": "show_command",
  "device": "spine1",
  "command": "show ip bgp summary",
  "decision": {
    "allowed": true,
    "reason": "read-only command approved",
    "risk": "low",
    "requires_approval": false
  },
  "result_summary": "success",
  "metadata": {}
}
```

This structure gives the team enough context to review the action without relying on memory or screenshots. That becomes important when several agents, clients, or engineers can call the same tool interface.

Observing the agent and tool layers

Observability is the difference between knowing that a demo worked once and knowing how a system behaves over time. A production team should watch the agent, the tool layer, and the backend integrations separately.

The most useful metrics are not complicated. Start with questions that operators already care about: are tools succeeding, are they slow, are commands being blocked, are users asking for unknown devices, and are errors increasing after a change?

Table 9.6 lists useful observability signals for a production-minded network agent:

Signal	What it tells you	Possible action
Tool call count	How often each tool is used	Identify popular or risky tools
Success rate	Whether tools are completing normally	Investigate drops after deployment
Blocked command count	How often policy blocks unsafe requests	Review training, prompts, or user intent
Unknown device requests	Whether users are asking for out-of-scope targets	Update inventory or clarify scope
Latency per tool	Which tools are slow	Tune backend calls or timeouts
Timeout rate	Whether backends are unreliable	Add retries, backoff, or alerts
Approval rate	How often risky actions are approved or denied	Review policy and operator workload
Model/tool mismatch errors	Whether the model asks for invalid tools or arguments	Improve tool descriptions and validation

Table 9.6: Observability signals for network agents

A system that cannot be observed cannot be trusted for operations. Before expanding scope, make sure the team can see what the agent is doing and where it fails.

Handling failure and rollback planning

Production failures are rarely dramatic in the way demos are. They are usually boring: a timeout, a missing key, a stale device name, a refused connection, an expired credential, or an output shape that changed after a software upgrade.

The safest response is to fail closed. If a policy check fails, do not execute the tool. If a parser cannot validate output, do not use it for a conclusion. If a backend times out, report uncertainty instead of inventing a result.

Table 9.7 maps common failure modes to safer responses:

Failure mode	Risk	Safer response
Unknown device	Tool may target the wrong system	Reject the request and return the approved device list
Unsupported command	Tool may change state or expose too much data	Block the command and explain the allowlist
Backend timeout	Agent may continue with missing evidence	Return a timeout error and mark the answer incomplete
Malformed output	Parser may accept bad data	Reject or retry with bounded attempts
Partial data	Conclusion may overstate certainty	Report what is known and what is missing
Approval denied	Action should not continue	Stop safely and log the decision
Unexpected write request	Agent may exceed scope	Block by default and require formal review

Table 9.7: Failure modes and safe responses

Rollback planning belongs with write actions, not after them. If the team cannot describe how to reverse a change, the agent should not execute that change automatically.

Using the production skeleton pattern

The production skeleton demo is `production_agent_skeleton.py` in `labs/lab6-production-readiness/`. It demonstrates another important production idea: keep the agent-facing contract stable while the backend implementation changes.

Run the demo from the repository root:

```
python3 labs/lab6-production-readiness/production_agent_skeleton.py
```

The mock backend returns data through the same agent-facing contract, while the real backend is intentionally a placeholder. A shortened output looks like this:

```
=== Mock backend demo ===
{
  "device": "leaf2",
  "summary": "BGP issue detected: 1/2 peers are established."
}

=== Real backend placeholder demo ===
{
  "device": "leaf2",
  "summary": "Device status check failed: RealNetworkBackend.device_status is not
implemented yet"
}
```

The placeholder is useful because it prevents accidental overpromising. The structure shows where a future SSH, controller API, NetBox, or NAPALM backend could be added, while the agent-facing method names and return shape remain stable.

Planning a staged rollout

The move from lab to production should be staged. The first production milestone should not be configuration changes; it should be controlled observation with logging and review.

Table 9.8 shows a practical rollout path for network agents:

Stage	What changes	Exit criteria
Local lab	Mock data and local tools only	Labs run reliably and outputs are understood

Stage	What changes	Exit criteria
Internal demo	Small team tests read-only workflows	Known issues are documented and tool output is reviewable
Read-only pilot	Approved users query approved real systems	Logs, access control, and failure handling are working
Recommendation mode	Agent suggests actions but does not execute them	Engineers trust evidence quality and review workflow
Approved action mode	Limited changes require human approval	Approvals, rollback notes, and audit trails are complete
Expanded production scope	More tools or devices are added gradually	Monitoring and ownership are mature enough for scale

Table 9.8: Staged rollout path for network agents

A staged rollout keeps the blast radius small. It also gives the team time to learn what the agent is good at and where it still needs stronger constraints.

Reviewing the production-readiness checklist

The repository includes a practical review sheet named `production_checklist.md` in `labs/lab6-production-readiness/`. Ready-to-copy production-readiness, runbook, feature flag, and go/no-go templates are also available under `docs/design-toolkit/`. These files are worth reviewing before connecting any agent-assisted workflow to real network systems.

The checklist covers scope, tool safety, secrets, human approval, observability, reliability, data quality, testing, change control, and go/no-go questions. That may sound like a lot, but these are the same concerns that already exist in network automation. Agents simply make the boundaries more important.

Before a pilot, the team should be able to answer these questions clearly:

- What is the exact use case and device scope?
- Which tools can the agent call automatically?
- Which tools require approval?
- What credentials are used, and where are they stored?

- What logs prove what the agent did?
- How are blocked requests reported?
- How does the system behave when a backend times out?
- Who owns the agent after deployment?
- How can the agent be disabled quickly?
- What evidence would we show after an incident review?

If the answers are weak, that is not failure. It means the system should stay in lab, demo, or read-only pilot mode until the gaps are closed.

Building a production review packet

A production review is easier when the information is already organized. Do not wait for a risk review meeting to discover that nobody knows which tools exist, which devices are in scope, or where the logs go.

Before a network agent enters a read-only pilot, prepare a small production review packet. This does not need to be a large document set. It needs to be clear enough that another engineer, security reviewer, or operations manager can understand the workflow without reading every line of code.

Table 9.9 lists the artifacts that make a review practical:

Review artifact	What it should contain	Why it helps
Use case summary	Problem, scope, users, and expected value	Prevents the agent from becoming a vague general tool
Tool inventory	Tool names, arguments, outputs, and owners	Makes the exposed capabilities visible
Device scope	Allowed devices, groups, environments, and exclusions	Keeps the blast radius small
Command policy	Allowed show commands and blocked command classes	Makes command safety reviewable

Review artifact	What it should contain	Why it helps
Access model	Who can call each tool and under what role	Connects the tool layer to authorization
Logging plan	Fields captured, retention period, and log destination	Supports audit and incident review
Failure plan	Timeout behavior, retries, blocked actions, and escalation path	Shows how the system fails safely
Disable plan	How to stop the agent, bridge, or tool server quickly	Gives operations a safety lever

Table 9.9: Production review packet for a network agent

The review packet is not bureaucracy for its own sake. It is how you make the system understandable to the people who will operate it when the original builder is not in the room.

Testing before a controlled pilot

A working happy path is not enough. Production readiness depends on how the tool behaves when inputs are wrong, devices are missing, services are slow, and users ask for something unsafe.

Start with unit tests around wrapper functions. Then test the mock workflow end to end. Then test failure cases deliberately. If the agent only works when every input is perfect, it is not ready for a pilot.

Useful tests include the following:

- Known good device requests, such as `device_status("spine1")`
- Unknown device requests, such as `device_status("core99")`
- Allowed read-only commands, such as `show ip bgp summary`
- Blocked commands, such as `configure terminal`
- Malformed tool arguments, such as missing `device` or invalid `count`
- Timeout simulations for backends that fail or respond slowly
- Partial data cases where one tool succeeds and another fails
- Model conclusion checks where the summary must match structured tool evidence

Table 9.10 organizes those tests into a simple readiness matrix:

Test area	Example test	Expected result
Device validation	Request `core99`	Tool rejects the device with a structured error
Command policy	Request `configure terminal`	Tool blocks the command and marks the risk as high
Read-only path	Request `show ip bgp summary`	Tool allows the command and logs the result
BGP evidence	Check `leaf2`	Agent reports 1/2 peers established and identifies the idle peer
Backend placeholder	Use `RealNetworkBackend`	Tool returns not implemented errors without pretending success
Log capture	Call any production wrapper	Audit event includes tool, device, decision, and result summary
Failure wording	Force partial data	Agent reports uncertainty instead of inventing a conclusion

Table 9.10: Production-readiness test matrix

These tests are not only for developers. They also give operations teams examples of what safe failure should look like. That makes reviews faster and support easier.

Writing an operations runbook

A production agent needs a runbook. The runbook explains how to start it, stop it, test it, monitor it, and escalate when something goes wrong. Without a runbook, the agent becomes another custom system that only one person knows how to operate.

The runbook should be short enough that an on-call engineer can use it during an incident. It should not require reading the source code to answer basic operational questions.

A useful runbook should include the sections shown in *Table 9.11*:

Runbook section	What to include	Example
Purpose	What the agent is intended to do	Read-only BGP and interface triage
Scope	Approved environments, devices, and users	Lab, staging, or selected production devices
Startup	Commands or service names used to start components	Start tool server, bridge, and UI if applicable
Health checks	How to confirm the service is working	Run wrapper tests or call a known safe tool
Logs	Where audit and application logs are stored	Log pipeline, file path, or SIEM index
Common failures	Known errors and first checks	Backend timeout, unknown device, blocked command
Escalation	Who owns the system and when to page them	Automation maintainer or NetOps owner
Disable path	How to stop the system safely	Disable service, revoke token, or remove route to tool server

Table 9.11: Runbook sections for a production network agent

A good runbook is part of the production boundary. It turns the agent from a personal project into something the team can support.

Using feature flags and kill switches

The fastest way to reduce operational risk is to make scope easy to narrow. A feature flag lets you enable or disable a capability without editing code. A kill switch lets the team stop the workflow quickly if something unexpected happens.

Feature flags are useful for staged rollout. You can enable `bgp_summary` for a small group first, then expand later. You can keep `show_command` disabled until command allowlists and logging are approved. You can keep write tools disabled until the team is ready for explicit approvals.

A simple configuration model might look like this:

```
{
  "tools": {
    "device_status": {"enabled": true},
    "bgp_summary": {"enabled": true},
    "show_command": {"enabled": true, "read_only_only": true},
    "configure_interface": {"enabled": false}
  },
  "global_kill_switch": false,
  "allowed_environment": "read_only_pilot"
}
```

This example is not a required format. It shows the idea: tool access should be controllable without changing prompts or redeploying the model. If the agent behaves unexpectedly, the team should have a fast way to reduce scope or stop the workflow.

Assigning ownership and support

Production readiness also has a people side. Someone must own the code, someone must own the tool policy, someone must review access, and someone must respond when the system fails. If ownership is unclear, the agent should not become a production dependency.

Ownership does not need to be complicated, but it should be explicit. *Table 9.12* shows a simple responsibility split:

Responsibility	Primary owner	What they review
Tool implementation	Automation engineer	Tool code, schemas, tests, and backend adapters
Network scope	Network engineering lead	Approved devices, commands, and operational boundaries
Access policy	Platform or security owner	Authentication, RBAC, service accounts, and tokens

Responsibility	Primary owner	What they review
Operations support	NOC or NetOps team	Runbook, alerts, escalation, and incident handling
Audit and compliance	Security or governance reviewer	Logs, retention, approvals, and evidence trail
Model behavior	Agent owner or AI platform team	Prompt behavior, model changes, and output review

Table 9.12: Ownership model for a production network agent

The exact team names may differ, but the principle is stable. Production agents need owners. If every issue is everyone's responsibility, then no issue is truly owned.

Defining acceptance criteria

Before a pilot starts, define what success looks like. Otherwise, the team may judge the agent by a few impressive demos instead of operational behavior over time.

Good acceptance criteria are measurable and practical. They should cover usefulness, safety, and operability. For example, a read-only pilot might require accurate evidence summaries, low tool error rates, complete audit logs, and no unauthorized command execution.

A pilot acceptance sheet can use criteria like these:

Criterion	Target for read-only pilot	How to measure it
Evidence quality	Final answers cite relevant tool evidence	Review sampled transcripts against logs
Tool safety	No unsafe commands are executed	Audit blocked and allowed command logs
Error handling	Failures return clear structured errors	Inject unknown devices and backend timeouts
Latency	Common tool paths complete within an agreed threshold	Track per-tool duration

Criterion	Target for read-only pilot	How to measure it
Audit completeness	Every tool call has a log event	Compare user requests to audit records
Operator usefulness	Engineers say summaries reduce triage time	Collect feedback during pilot shifts

Table 9.13: Acceptance criteria for a read-only pilot

Acceptance criteria keep the pilot grounded. The agent does not need to solve every outage. It needs to demonstrate that it can help safely, consistently, and visibly within a defined scope.

Creating a production-readiness worksheet

The final review works best when each question has an owner and evidence. A question such as "*Are we logging tool calls?*" is useful, but it is not enough. The review should ask who owns the answer and where the proof lives.

A production-readiness worksheet turns the checklist into a working document. It can live in a ticket, a wiki page, or a repository file. The format matters less than the discipline: every major risk should have an answer, an owner, and evidence.

Table 9.14 gives a practical worksheet format readers can adapt for their own agent projects:

Review question	Owner	Evidence to attach
What use case is approved for the first pilot?	Agent owner	Written scope statement and excluded use cases
Which devices are in scope?	Network engineering lead	Device allowlist or inventory group
Which tools are enabled?	Automation engineer	Tool inventory and configuration file
Which commands are allowlisted?	Network engineering lead	Approved command list and policy note
Who can call the tools?	Platform or security owner	RBAC mapping and service account details

Review question	Owner	Evidence to attach
Where do audit logs go?	Operations owner	Log destination, retention setting, and sample log event
How do we disable the agent quickly?	Operations owner	Runbook section or tested disable procedure
How will the pilot be evaluated?	Project owner	Acceptance criteria and review date

Table 9.14: Production-readiness worksheet for a network agent pilot

This worksheet should be completed before a pilot, not after a problem. If a row has no owner or no evidence, that is a sign that the pilot needs more preparation.

Preparing an approval record

If the system ever moves beyond read-only recommendations, approvals need to be captured as structured records. The approval record should contain enough context for a human to make a decision and enough detail for an audit trail later.

Even if the first production pilot stays read-only, it is useful to design the approval shape early. That way, future write-capable workflows are built around review rather than adding review after the fact.

A simple approval record might look like this:

```
{
  "approval_id": "CHG-20491",
  "requested_by": "network-agent",
  "reviewer": "senior-netops-engineer",
  "target_device": "leaf2",
  "proposed_action": "clear bgp neighbor 10.1.2.2",
  "risk": "high",
  "evidence": {
    "bgp_state": "Idle",
    "prefixes": 0,
    "last_checked": "2026-06-28T18:40:00Z"
  },
  "rollback_plan": "No configuration change. Verify session state after action.",
```

```
    "decision": "pending"
}
```

This example is intentionally structured. The reviewer can see the target, the proposed action, the evidence, the risk, and the rollback thinking. A real implementation would also include links to the ticket, logs, user identity, and policy decision.

Avoiding production shortcuts

The pressure to move quickly is real. Once a demo looks useful, people naturally ask whether it can do more. That is exactly when shortcuts become tempting.

The most common shortcuts are easy to recognize. Someone wants to use broad device credentials because creating a read-only service account takes time. Someone wants to expose `run_command()` because it is faster than defining five narrow tools. Someone wants to skip logging because the demo output is visible in the terminal. Those shortcuts save time early and create problems later.

Use these questions when a shortcut is proposed:

- Does this increase the blast radius?
- Would this make an incident harder to investigate?
- Does this bypass an existing change or access control process?
- Can this be replaced by a narrower read-only tool?
- Can this wait until after the pilot has produced evidence?
- Would we be comfortable documenting this shortcut in the runbook?

If the shortcut is hard to justify in writing, it is probably not ready for production. The point of the first pilot is to learn safely, not to prove that the agent can do everything at once.

Connecting the chapter back to the book's journey

This chapter is the last main step in the journey we started in *Chapter 1*. We began by defining AI agents as systems made from models, code, tools, context, and guardrails. The production version of that definition has not changed. The guardrails simply become more explicit.

The full path now looks like this:

- *Chapter 1* defined agents and the operational problem they help solve
- *Chapter 2* established local LLM behavior and setup
- *Chapter 3* introduced structured prompt design with RACE
- *Chapter 4* turned raw network output into validated JSON

- *Chapter 5* added application-managed memory
- *Chapter 6* introduced controlled tool calling
- *Chapter 7* used tools in a troubleshooting investigation
- *Chapter 8* exposed reusable tools through MCP
- *Chapter 9* wrapped those ideas in production-readiness controls

That sequence matters. A production network agent is not a single prompt. It is the result of many boring, necessary layers: tool boundaries, validation, logs, approvals, and human ownership.

Final go/no-go review

Before moving beyond read-only use, run one final go/no-go review. This should be a meeting or checklist that includes the people who will own the tool after the demo is over. The question is not whether the demo looked good. The question is whether the system can be operated safely.

Use these questions as the final review gate:

1. What is the worst thing this agent can do with its current permissions?
2. Can we detect that behavior quickly?
3. Can we stop the workflow safely?
4. Can we explain the agent output using logged tool evidence?
5. Can an engineer override, reject, or challenge the recommendation?
6. Are secrets protected from prompts, logs, and repositories?
7. Does every risky action require approval?
8. Would we be comfortable showing the audit trail after an incident?

If the answer to any of those questions is unclear, keep the workflow read-only. The right time to slow down is before the agent has permission to do something expensive.

Summary

In this chapter, we moved from lab functionality to production readiness. We looked at the boundaries that need to exist before a network agent is evaluated against real infrastructure: authentication, authorization, secrets handling, validation, approval gates, logging, observability, failure handling, and staged rollout planning.

We used the Lab 6 folder as a reference pattern, not as a finished production platform. The safety wrapper demo showed how to approve known devices, block unsafe commands, and log tool decisions. The production skeleton showed how to keep the agent-facing contract stable while the backend can later change from mock data to a real network source.

We also covered the operational pieces that make an agent supportable: review packets, test matrices, runbooks, feature flags, kill switches, ownership, acceptance criteria, readiness worksheets, and approval records. Those topics may feel less exciting than tool calling, but they are what separate an impressive demo from a system a team can responsibly evaluate.

The key takeaway is simple: an agent becomes trustworthy only when the system around it is trustworthy. Useful answers are not enough. Engineers need evidence, boundaries, logs, ownership, and a safe way to say no.

At this point, you have completed the main journey of the book: from local LLM calls to production-readiness thinking. Do not give the agent more power immediately. Test carefully, keep the first pilot read-only, and let operational evidence decide what to automate next. *Appendix A* provides reusable checklists and templates for your own network agent projects.

Get this book's PDF version and more

10

Unlock Your Exclusive Benefits

Your copy of this book includes the following exclusive benefits:

DRM-Free PDF Version

Download DRM-free PDF and ePub copies of this book.

7-Day Packt Library Access

Get 7-day unlimited access to 8,000+ books and videos. No credit card required.

Available for first-time Packt+ trial users only.

Next-Gen Reader Access

Read this book on Packt Reader with progress sync, dark mode and note-taking.

Follow the guide below to unlock them. The process takes only a few minutes and needs to be completed once.

Unlock this Book's Free Benefits in three Easy Steps

Step 1

Keep your purchase invoice ready for *Step 3*. If you have a physical copy, scan it using your phone and save it as a PDF, JPG, or PNG.

For more help on finding your invoice, visit `packtpub.com/en-us/unlock?step=1`.

> **Note**
>
> If you bought this book directly from Packt, no invoice is required. After *Step 2*, you can access your exclusive content right away.

Step 2

Scan the QR code or go to `packtpub.com/unlock`.

On the page that opens (similar to *Figure 10.1* on desktop), search for this book by name and select the correct edition.

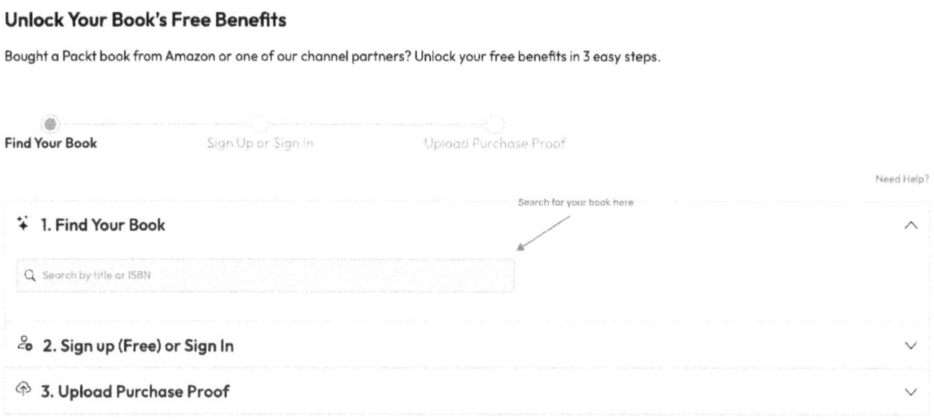

Figure 10.1: Packt unlock landing page on desktop

Step 3

After selecting your book, sign in to your Packt account or create one for free. Then upload your invoice (PDF, PNG, or JPG, up to 10 MB). Follow the on-screen instructions to finish the process.

Need Help

If you get stuck and need help, visit `packtpub.com/unlock-benefits/help` for a detailed FAQ on how to find your invoices and more. This QR code will take you to the help page.

> **Note**
>
> If you are still facing issues, reach out to `customercare@packt.com`.

Appendix A
AI Network Agent Design Toolkit

This appendix turns the book's main ideas into reusable design artifacts. Use it when you want to move from a lab agent to a reviewed operational prototype. The templates are intentionally practical: each one helps you define scope, validate outputs, document tool behavior, review safety controls, or prepare a read-only pilot.

The appendix is not meant to replace the chapters. It is a working pack that helps you apply the chapter concepts with less guesswork. You can copy these checklists into a design document, ticket, wiki page, or review packet and adapt them for your own environment. Ready-to-copy versions of these templates and worksheets are available in the book repository under `docs/design-toolkit/`.

Use this appendix in three situations:

- Before building an agent, to decide whether an agent is the right tool for the problem
- During implementation, to keep prompts, tools, validation, and memory consistent
- Before a pilot, to review access, logging, approvals, rollback, and operational ownership

The safest path is still the one used throughout the book: start local, stay read-only, validate every tool result, show evidence, and keep the engineer in control.

Book concepts mapped to design artifacts

The chapters build the agent step by step. This appendix maps that journey to the artifacts a team should create before evaluating a network agent beyond a local lab.

Book concept	Design artifact to create	How the artifact helps
Agent use case	Use-case brief	Prevents the agent from becoming a vague general assistant
RACE prompts	Prompt worksheet	Keeps role, anchors, context, and expected output testable
Structured parsing	Schema and validation checklist	Stops malformed or invented output from moving downstream
Memory	Context policy	Defines what history is kept, summarized, or cleared
Tool calling	Tool inventory and safety matrix	Shows which functions the model can request and what is blocked
Troubleshooting loop	Evidence record and response template	Ties final answers to tool results
MCP tooling	Tool contract worksheet	Stabilizes names, inputs, outputs, and error behavior
Production readiness	Pilot checklist and runbook	Makes the workflow reviewable and supportable

Table A.1: Mapping book concepts to reusable design artifacts

If you create only one document for a pilot, combine the use-case brief, tool inventory, evidence model, logging plan, and go/no-go checklist. That gives reviewers enough information to understand both value and risk.

Use-case fit scorecard

Not every workflow needs an agent. Use the scorecard in *Table A.2* before starting implementation. If the task is deterministic, already automated, or unsafe without human review, a conventional script or runbook may be the better choice.

Question	Good agent signal	Stop or redesign signal
Does the task require context from more than one source?	The agent needs alerts, device state, logs, topology, or tickets together	One command or one API call already answers the question
Does the next step depend on evidence?	The workflow changes based on BGP, interface, log, or reachability results	The workflow is always the same sequence of steps
Can the first version stay read-only?	The agent can add value by observing, summarizing, and recommending	The first useful version must change configuration
Can outputs be validated?	Tool results have schemas, allowed values, or deterministic checks	The answer depends only on free-form model judgment
Can engineers review the evidence?	The system can show tool calls, inputs, outputs, and final reasoning	The answer is a black box with no audit trail
Is there a clear owner?	A named team owns tool policy, code, logs, and support	Nobody owns it after the demo

Table A.2: Agent use-case fit scorecard

Use-case brief template

The use-case brief should be short. Its job is to make the first pilot narrow enough to review.

```
agent_use_case:
  name: "Read-only BGP triage assistant"
  problem: "Engineers spend time collecting BGP and interface evidence after
```

```
alerts."
  users: ["NOC engineer", "network operator"]
  first_scope: "Read-only triage for approved spine and leaf devices"
  excluded_scope:
    - "Configuration changes"
    - "Session resets"
    - "Unapproved devices"
  expected_value:
    - "Collect device, BGP, interface, and reachability evidence"
    - "Produce a concise troubleshooting summary"
    - "Suggest next checks for an engineer"
  success_measure:
    - "Final answer matches tool evidence"
    - "Every tool call is logged"
    - "No blocked command is executed"
```

RACE prompt worksheet

The RACE framework from Chapter 3 works best when the prompt is treated as a testable asset. Use *Table A.3* to create a prompt that can be reviewed before it is added to code.

RACE element	What to write	NetOps example
Role	The operational perspective the model should use	You are a network automation engineer extracting facts from CLI output
Anchors	Small input and output examples that show the target pattern	Show one interface input and the exact JSON shape expected
Context	The relevant device, vendor, command, limits, and constraints	This is Arista EOS output from a read-only command
Expected output	Exact format, fields, missing-value rules, and no-extra-text rules	Return one JSON object only; use null for missing values

Table A.3: RACE prompt worksheet

Reusable RACE prompt skeleton

Use the following skeleton when you need a reusable prompt structure for a read-only NetOps task:

```
ROLE:
You are a network automation assistant helping with read-only NetOps tasks.

ANCHORS:
Example input:
<short realistic input>

Example output:
<exact JSON or response shape>

CONTEXT:
Use only the supplied data.
Do not infer live state that is not present in the input.
The workflow is read-only.

EXPECTED OUTPUT:
Return the requested format only.
Do not use markdown fences.
Use null for missing values.
Do not invent device names, counters, neighbors, or causes.

TASK:
<the specific user request or data to process>
```

Keep prompts in version-controlled files when they influence automation. A small prompt change can change system behavior, so prompts should be reviewed like code.

Structured-output and validation checklist

Structured output is useful only when the application validates it. Before a model response feeds another tool, dashboard, ticket, or agent step, apply the checks in *Table A.4*.

Validation check	What to confirm	Example
JSON parse	The response can be parsed without manual cleanup	No prose before or after the JSON object

Validation check	What to confirm	Example
Required keys	Every required field exists	interface, admin_status, oper_status, ip_address, mtu
Allowed values	Fields use expected values	state is Established, Idle, Active, or unknown
Data types	Numbers, strings, arrays, and nulls match the schema	prefixes_received is an integer
Source grounding	Values appear in the raw input or tool result	Do not invent a MAC address or neighbor IP
Uncertainty handling	Missing or ambiguous data is explicit	Use null or unknown instead of guessing
Failure path	Invalid output returns a controlled error	Do not continue silently after validation fails

Table A.4: Structured-output validation checklist

Minimal schema checklist

Use the following checklist to define the required fields and validation rules for a structured response:

```
schema_review:
  object_name: "bgp_summary"
  required_fields:
    - device
    - total_peers
    - established_peers
    - neighbors
  allowed_states:
    - Established
    - Idle
    - Active
    - Connect
    - unknown
  validation_rules:
    - "established_peers must be less than or equal to total_peers"
```

```
    - "each neighbor must include ip, state, and prefixes"
    - "final answer must mention any neighbor not in Established state"
```

Testing different models

The examples in this book use specific local models so that the labs remain consistent and easier to follow. After you complete the labs, you can try the same prompts, parsing tasks, and agent workflows with other models to compare which one gives the most accurate and useful results for your environment. When testing a new model, keep the prompt, input data, expected output format, and validation checks the same so that the comparison is fair. Review whether the model produces valid structured output, uses the available tools correctly, explains its findings with evidence, and avoids unsupported conclusions. Also compare practical factors such as latency, system resource use, repeatability, and how often human review is needed.

When comparing models, check the following:

- Does the model follow the expected output format?
- Does it preserve key network facts from the input?
- Does it avoid inventing device state, routes, logs, or tool results?
- Does it call the right tool for the task?
- Does it explain findings with evidence?
- Does it behave consistently across repeated runs?
- Does it run fast enough on your available hardware?
- Does it still require the same validation, logging, and approval controls?

Memory and context policy

Memory helps a troubleshooting assistant carry context across turns, but it also creates risk. Old context can become stale, misleading, or too large. Define what the application stores and what it sends back to the model.

Memory decision	Recommended starting point	Why it matters
Session history	Keep recent user and assistant turns for the active investigation	Supports follow-up questions without overloading context

Memory decision	Recommended starting point	Why it matters
Older context	Summarize older turns when the session gets long	Controls token growth and reduces stale detail
Tool results	Store raw results separately from the model response	Allows deterministic checks and audit review
Sensitive data	Avoid storing secrets, credentials, or unnecessary payloads	Reduces data exposure risk
Reset behavior	Provide a clear reset or new-case command	Stops old context from polluting a new investigation
Retention	Define how long history and evidence are kept	Supports privacy, audit, and storage control

Table A.5: Memory and context policy checklist

Tool inventory and safety matrix

Every tool the model can request should be listed before it is exposed. The inventory should explain what the tool does, which arguments it accepts, what it returns, and what safety rule blocks bad requests.

Tool	Purpose	Safety rule
`device_status(device)`	Return inventory and health for one known device	Reject unknown devices
`interface_status(device, interface=None)`	Return one interface or all interfaces for a device	Validate device and optional interface
`bgp_summary(device)`	Return BGP peer state and prefix counts	Validate device and return structured errors
`ping(target, count=4)`	Run bounded reachability checks	Limit count and reject unsafe targets

Tool	Purpose	Safety rule
`show_command(device, command)`	Run approved read-only show commands	Allowlist commands and block configuration mode
`topology()`	Return known topology relationships	Return static or approved inventory data only

Table A.6: Tool inventory and safety matrix

Tool contract template

Use the following template to document the contract for a controlled network tool:

```
tool_contract:
  name: "bgp_summary"
  owner: "Network automation team"
  purpose: "Return BGP neighbor state for an approved device"
  arguments:
    device:
      type: "string"
      required: true
      validation: "must exist in approved device allowlist"
  returns:
    device: "string"
    total_peers: "integer"
    established_peers: "integer"
    neighbors: "array"
  blocked_when:
    - "device is unknown"
    - "backend times out"
  logs:
    - "user_or_client_id"
    - "tool"
    - "device"
    - "decision.allowed"
    - "duration_ms"
```

A tool contract should change slowly. If another client depends on the tool name, arguments, or return shape, treat changes as compatibility decisions, not casual refactoring.

Evidence record for troubleshooting agents

A good troubleshooting answer should be tied to evidence. The model can write the summary, but the application should keep a structured record of what was checked and what looked unhealthy.

```
{
  "case_id": "INC-12345",
  "user_request": "Check whether leaf2 has any issues",
  "target_device": "leaf2",
  "evidence": {
    "device_status": {
      "tool": "device_status",
      "status": "up",
      "source": "mock_network_devices"
    },
    "bgp_summary": {
      "tool": "bgp_summary",
      "total_peers": 2,
      "established_peers": 1,
      "unhealthy_neighbors": [
        {"ip": "10.1.2.2", "state": "Idle", "prefixes": 0}
      ]
    },
    "interface_status": {
      "tool": "interface_status",
      "down_interfaces": [
        {"name": "Ethernet3", "description": "server_rack_2"}
      ]
    }
  },
  "validation": {
    "bgp_issue_present": true,
    "down_interface_present": true,
    "final_answer_must_mention": ["10.1.2.2", "Ethernet3"]
  }
}
```

Troubleshooting response template

Use this answer shape when the agent is reporting an investigation. It keeps the response useful without pretending the investigation is complete.

```
Finding:
<short conclusion based on tool evidence>

Evidence:
- <confirmed fact from tool result>
- <unhealthy or suspicious signal>
- <missing or uncertain data, if any>

Likely cause:
<careful hypothesis. Use "may be related" when the tool data is incomplete.>

Next checks:
- <specific check the engineer should run or approve>
- <specific log, peer, interface, or route to verify>

Unknowns:
- <what the agent did not verify>
```

This structure is useful during incidents because it separates facts from hypotheses. It also gives reviewers a way to compare the final answer with the evidence record.

MCP tool contract worksheet

When tools move behind an MCP server, the tool name, arguments, and return shape become reusable contracts. *Table A.7* can be used before exposing a tool to multiple clients:

Contract item	**Question to answer**	**Example**
Public tool name	What name will clients discover?	bgp_summary
Internal implementation	Which wrapper or backend function runs?	safe_bgp_summary(device)
Arguments	Which inputs are required or optional?	device is required; count defaults to 4

Contract item	Question to answer	Example
Validation	What is rejected before execution?	Unknown devices and non-show commands
Return shape	What keys can clients depend on?	device, total_peers, established_peers, neighbors
Error shape	How are failures returned?	structured error with allowed false and reason
Logging	What does the server or bridge record?	tool, args, decision, status, duration
Versioning	How will breaking changes be handled?	new tool name or versioned schema

Table A.7: MCP tool contract worksheet

Production readiness checklist

A production-ready network agent is not just a model with better prompts. It is a system with boundaries, ownership, logs, approvals, failure handling, and a way to stop safely. Use *Table A. 8* before a read-only pilot.

Readiness area	Minimum expectation for a read-only pilot	Evidence to attach
Scope	Use case, users, devices, and excluded actions are documented	Scope statement or ticket
Authentication	Callers are identified before tool access	Identity provider or service account details
Authorization	Tool access is limited by role or allowlist	RBAC mapping
Secrets	Credentials are not in prompts, code, or logs	Secrets storage plan

Readiness area	Minimum expectation for a read-only pilot	Evidence to attach
Validation	Inputs and outputs are checked before use	Schema or validation code
Logging	Every tool call creates an audit event	Sample log event
Observability	Tool errors, latency, and blocked requests are visible	Dashboard or metric list
Failure behavior	Timeouts and invalid outputs fail closed	Failure test results
Approval gates	Write actions are disabled or require review	Approval policy
Disable path	The workflow can be stopped quickly	Runbook step or kill switch
Ownership	Code, tool policy, and operations support have named owners	Owner list

Table A.8: Production readiness checklist for a read-only pilot

Audit event template

Use the following template to record a tool call in a reviewable audit format:

```
{
  "timestamp": "2026-06-28T18:36:38Z",
  "user_or_client_id": "noc-operator-1",
  "tool": "show_command",
  "device": "spine1",
  "command": "show ip bgp summary",
  "decision": {
    "allowed": true,
    "reason": "read-only command approved",
    "risk": "low",
    "requires_approval": false
```

```
  },
  "result_summary": "success",
  "duration_ms": 184,
  "approval_id": null
}
```

Read-only pilot acceptance criteria

Acceptance criteria keep a pilot grounded. A pilot should not be judged by one impressive demo. It should be judged by repeated behavior inside a defined scope.

Criterion	Target	How to measure it
Evidence quality	Final answers cite or reflect relevant tool evidence	Sample transcripts against tool logs
Tool safety	No unsafe command is executed	Audit allowed and blocked command events
Validation	Malformed outputs do not move downstream	Validation failure tests
Latency	Common read-only checks finish within the agreed threshold	Per-tool duration metrics
Audit completeness	Every tool call has a log event	Compare user requests with audit records
Operator usefulness	Engineers say summaries reduce triage time or context gathering	Pilot feedback form
Scope control	Requests outside scope are rejected clearly	Out-of-scope test cases
Disable readiness	The team can stop the workflow quickly	Tested disable procedure

Table A.9: Acceptance criteria for a read-only pilot

Operations runbook template

A runbook turns the agent from a personal experiment into something a team can support. Keep the first runbook short and operational.

Runbook section	What to include	Example
Purpose	What the agent is intended to support	Read-only BGP and interface triage
Scope	Approved environments, users, devices, and exclusions	Selected lab or pilot devices only
Startup	Commands, services, or deployment steps	Start MCP server and bridge
Health checks	Known safe calls that confirm the workflow is working	Call device_status for spine1
Logs	Where audit and application logs are stored	Log pipeline, file path, or SIEM index
Common failures	Known symptoms and first checks	Unknown device, backend timeout, blocked command
Escalation	Who owns support and when to contact them	Network automation owner or NetOps lead
Disable path	How to stop the workflow or reduce scope	Disable service, revoke token, or use global kill switch

Table A.10: Operations runbook template for a network agent

Feature flag and kill switch template

Use the following template to define which tools are enabled and how the workflow can be stopped:

```
{
  "global_kill_switch": false,
  "allowed_environment": "read_only_pilot",
  "tools": {
    "device_status": {"enabled": true},
    "bgp_summary": {"enabled": true},
    "interface_status": {"enabled": true},
    "show_command": {
      "enabled": true,
      "read_only_only": true
    },
    "configure_interface": {"enabled": false}
  }
}
```

Go/no-go review

Use the final review in *Table A.11* before expanding beyond a local lab or internal demo. If any answer is unclear, keep the workflow read-only or keep it in the lab until the gap is closed.

Review question	Go signal	No-go signal
What is the worst thing the agent can do with current permissions?	The worst case is understood and bounded	The team cannot describe the blast radius
Can we detect unsafe or unexpected behavior?	Logs and alerts show tool calls, failures, and blocked actions	Behavior is visible only in terminal output
Can we stop the workflow quickly?	Disable path is documented and tested	Stopping requires code changes or unknown manual steps
Can we explain the final answer from tool evidence?	Evidence record and logs support the response	The final answer cannot be traced to inputs

Review question	Go signal	No-go signal
Are secrets protected?	Secrets are outside prompts, code, and logs	Credentials are copied into prompts or repo files
Does every risky action require approval?	Write actions are disabled or approval-gated	The agent can change state without review
Who owns the system after the pilot?	Owners are named for code, operations, and policy	Ownership is informal or unclear

Table A.11: Final go/no-go review questions

A useful network agent does not need to be dramatic. It needs to be scoped, observable, evidence-based, and safe to stop. Use this appendix as a working checklist, and let operational evidence decide when the system is ready for more responsibility.

Other Books You May Enjoy

AI Networking Cookbook

Eric Chou

ISBN: 978-1-80580-799-5

- Understand the AI LLM landscape and key parameters for networking tasks
- Create OpenAI-enabled scripts for daily network engineering workflows
- Master prompt engineering techniques for improved AI outputs
- Build local LLMs using Ollama for network applications
- Chain language models with LangChain for complex network solutions
- Develop AI application frontends using the Streamlit framework
- Design robust backends for network AI applications
- Build an end-to-end network copilot by integrating all the techniques you've learned

Agentic AI for Platform Engineering

Tiago Miguel Reichert, Lucas Soriano Alves Duarte, Jaime Nagase

ISBN: 978-1-80638-665-9

- Integrate GenAI and RAG into internal developer platforms
- Build conversational interfaces for infrastructure-as-code generation
- Implement AI-powered observability with agentic self-healing
- Design and deploy multi-agent systems for autonomous operations
- Apply MCP to connect AI tools with organizational knowledge systems
- Secure AI-enhanced platforms against prompt injection and identity threats
- Govern agentic AI with human-in-the-loop patterns and compliance frameworks
- Evaluate build vs. buy decisions for AI platform tooling

Packt is searching for authors like you

If you're interested in becoming an author for Packt, please visit `https://authors.packt.com` and apply today. We have worked with thousands of developers and tech professionals, just like you, to help them share their insight with the global tech community. You can make a general application, apply for a specific hot topic that we are recruiting an author for, or submit your own idea.

Share your thoughts

Now you've finished *Building AI Agents for Network Operations*, we'd love to hear your thoughts! Scan the QR code below to go straight to the Amazon review page for this book and share your feedback or leave a review on the site that you purchased it from.

`https://packt.link/r/1-808-34683-1`

Your review is important to us and the tech community and will help us make sure we're delivering excellent quality content.

Index

N

O

www.ingramcontent.com/pod-product-compliance
Lightning Source LLC
LaVergne TN
LVHW060034210926
848481LV00013B/3862
9781808346835